Moon River and Me:

A Personal Account of Loss, Grief & Depression

Written by

Stewart Patterson

Dedicated to the life and memory of

William 'Billy' Patterson

11/07/1950 – 16/03/2017

Missed every day.

The wee birdies sing and the wildflowers spring,

and in sunshine the waters are sleeping.

But the broken heart it kens nae second spring again,

though the waeful may cease frae their greetin.

Introduction

The Leap of Faith

Sad. Depressed. Shocked. Numb. Suicidal. Detached. Broken.

Take your pick.

There are a million and one words I could use to *try* and explain how I have felt over these past few years. The highs and the many lows. The truth is it is too complicated and overwhelming to be explained by words alone. I have tried to convey it to family, friends, work colleagues – even casual acquaintances and strangers – but I simply cannot describe what is going on in my head and in my heart.

It's important to note that this is my own personal experience of grief, trauma, and depression. Everyone's journey is unique, so please forgive me for being self-indulgent at times. It's what I've needed to help heal. For me, I wouldn't have known what Depression was if it kicked me on the backside

I genuinely didn't know I had a 'Mental Health' until it was compromised. From a place of both ignorance and naivety, I can say honestly that I did not understand why people couldn't 'snap out of it'.

I was an optimist, a fighter. Always had a joke and a smile. In short - I was 'normal' and I was happy.

I was first diagnosed with Depression in November 2017, 8 months after my Dad died suddenly. Prior to my diagnosis, I obviously knew I was feeling 'low', but I was in mental anguish, I was grieving. I did not consider that I had issues beyond the obvious grief. I certainly did not think I had an illness. In my mind, I did not have to be a rocket scientist to know that losing my Dad would make me feel terrible!

It's how it was supposed to feel, surely. Even when I started to have suicidal and unusual thoughts, I was so shocked and numbed by the sudden loss that the seriousness nor the shift in my perception of the world registered with me.

The impact of my Dad's death on my Mental Health was obviously immediate due to the onset of grief. Over the following months, my Mental Health deteriorated subtly. Of course, 'Subtly' is completely the wrong word to use because, in normal circumstances, there was nothing subtle about it.

But my day-to-day struggles with grief allowed the Depression to grow without detection. Or rather, without identification. It's impossible to say when my grief stopped, and the

Depression began. Impossible because I recognise now that they're both one and the same. The grief triggered my Depression and feeds it. The Depression makes the grief worse, makes me question my entire life and purpose. It really is an inseparable and vicious cycle.

The feelings felt are so personal and deep (and new). So extreme. I've started to put these words down on paper countless times, then stopped and revisited more times than I can remember. It's been difficult to know where to start and truthfully, it's been difficult to know what to share with you. How deep and honest I should be and whether it's good for me to lay-out my vulnerabilities and struggles for people, my family, to see.

I have struggled with accepting this new 'version' of myself and have worried, and still worry, that people will see me as a burden. Ultimately, I'm so aware of how I've felt about myself that I've been so terrified that other people see me in the same way. The thought of pushing people away or people giving up on me has been a real concern.

I've always been a rational person (or at least I like to think I have!). But this is the illness. This is one of the areas where it has attacked me personally. It's made me grow tired of myself and rationally, at least in my mind, it's not been much of a stretch to imagine that my friends and family could also grow tired of me. That I am a burden, and not a positive presence in their lives anymore.

And there lies the conundrum. I'm glad to say that the previous 'version' of me isn't totally gone. He's in there somewhere. And his definition of rational thinking is different. He acknowledges the concern of abandonment but also knows that he's surrounded by love. People that love him, care about him and would do anything to help him.

So, this book is a collaboration of sorts – between the Dr Jekyll and Mr Hyde in my head. The part affected by the illness and the part that's fighting to survive. At the time of writing this, I've come to a reluctant truce and realisation - that I cannot separate the two.

They co-exist. In every thought, in every action. Therefore, I cannot write this without being honest with you. I have to open myself up and yes, be vulnerable. This new version is taking a leap of faith that some good will come from sharing this. And the old version is hoping that it helps him get better, take back control.

This control or the sense of controlling one's well-being has been difficult to comprehend. I never consciously felt 'in control' previously, but I have certainly felt 'not in control'. I'm at the mercy of my medication, triggers and the Demons that now exist in my head. I want to be happy – more than anything.

However, what that looks like is an unknown. Is this as good as it gets? Am I destined to exist like this for the rest of my life? Hanging in at times? I'm hopeful but afraid of waking up in 10 years feeling the same. This worry overwhelms and panics me.

During my early days of Depression, I read some books and articles and yes, I could relate to them......but only to a point. Then they'd lose me. Most of those poor souls had struggled with Depression for most of their adult lives, if not since their adolescence or sometimes earlier. Sometimes it was an accumulation of everyday stresses that built up over years before a breakdown.

But that *wasn't* me. It wasn't my experience. In my mind at the time, I'm Depressed because of one event that changed my life forever, for the worse. An unbearable pain and the devastation that it's left behind. I lost my Dad suddenly when I was 31 years old and from that moment, that Trauma, I have spiralled into this Depression. I have come to realise however that I misjudged.

Like in my experiences, this book may not help you. Like me, you may connect to some degree, but it doesn't quite capture why or how you feel. But for those who can relate – I hope you can take something, anything positive from reading this.

My Depression wasn't obvious to me, or even expected. Despite losing Dad, I didn't anticipate Depression because, I suppose, I had no comprehension of what it was. In my naive mind, my Depression came from that loss alone. If I could deal with the loss, then my Depression was cured. Simple and uncomplicated. However, nothing is ever that simple.

My journey has unearthed resentments and pain that were previously, seemingly insignificant. This new landscape and context, as well as my new state of mind, has found new ways to interpret the past and sometimes torment me. The loss of not only my beloved Dad but also the loss of happiness. The loss of the life I had. The damage to the quality of life. The damage to the family unit. The pain I see my Mum and siblings in.

I'm not an author. I've never written anything in my life! I doubt I have any kind of talent for it! But I've felt compelled to put my thoughts, feelings, ups and downs out there for people to see. During my battle with this Illness, one overwhelming theme keeps re-occurring – that people are good. People care. And not just the ones that are 'supposed to'. Without all of those people, I might not have gotten this far. Of course, my hope for writing this is to aid in my recovery. But that's not the only reason.

I do hope that someone, somewhere can find it helpful. That someone, somewhere feeling the same as I did and do, can take even the smallest comfort from knowing that they aren't alone. That they're 'normal'. I **know** there are countless numbers of people out there enduring this same Illness. Maybe for different reasons, or with similar but different challenges.

One day at a time is a bit of a cliché but it really is my 'safe mode' and has helped me dial that pressure back. I still have hope. It hasn't always been obvious but at the same time, it's never left.

'

PART ONE:
EARLY LIFE

Chapter I

Good Old Days

1985 – A year to Remember! The wreck of the Titanic was discovered by Bob Ballard and his team, the Live Aid concerts brought the World's attention to the famine in Ethiopia and Dr. Emmett Brown invented time travel. Significant and memorable events (OK Dr. Emmett Brown might be fictional – but I've loved Back to the Future my entire life so I can't mention 1985 without mentioning the Doc!). Oh, it was also the July of that year that I was born.

Born in Possilpark, located in the Northeast of Glasgow, to William ('Billy') & Mary Patterson. I was their 2nd child together (and 2nd son) joining my brother Wesley ('Wes' Born 1979). Both my parents had been married previously and my Dad had an older son, Robert ('Robin' Born 1974) from his previous marriage

Despite not having the same Mother, we were very much a blended family. My sister, Honor, arrived in 1987 to complete our Family unit and we moved a little bit further west, to Drumchapel, where we settled until my early teens.

Drumchapel & Possilpark aren't affluent areas of Glasgow. Indeed, at that time they were at the other end of the spectrum, where unemployment numbers were high, poverty was common and the need for Social Housing was always on the rise. We lived in an unusual Glasgow City Council home as it was actually two different tenement flats that had been converted and combined to fashion out a Maisonette type home. It was cool!

During our time in Drumchapel and my early years, my Dad worked as a Security Guard working 60+ hour weeks! This allowed my Mum to take the domestic responsibilities, so she stayed at home and looked after us. As well as myself, Honor and Wesley, Robin would visit and stay on alternate days from his Mum's, and my elderly paternal Grandmother also lived with us. Mum did a wonderful job. We weren't well off by any stretch of the imagination, but my Mum and Dad worked hard to provide for us.

I'm lucky. I certainly look back warmly on my childhood and long for the uncomplicated days before the serious business of life. We never ever went abroad for a holiday. Even as an adult, one of my dreams was to finally have a holiday abroad with my parents. I eventually managed to realise that dream with my Mum, but not my Dad.

Regardless, I absolutely loved our summer holidays at home. We were a very active family, all owning bikes and using them every day. My Dad would even cycle to work and despite both my parents being smokers, they seemed to be fitter and healthier than most of the other parents I knew from School or in the community.

Every summer, sometimes several times per summer, we'd cycle as a family from Drumchapel to Loch Lomond. It was wonderful. Such lovely memories to have. So much so that as a Dad of 3 boys myself now, I'd love to recreate those memories with them.

We'd cycle for a few miles then stop for a break at our regular stops. Stopping at harbours on the way for a sandwich and a laugh with the regular faces we'd see cycle the paths. I felt so happy and safe. It genuinely does give me such a content feeling in my core and brings a smile to my face thinking about those days even now.

I remember one time when I had cycled to Loch Lomond with my Dad and brothers. It was a beautiful summer's day and we had stopped for lunch at a local pub. My Dad and oldest brother had a beer with lunch, and we were all in high spirits. On the way home, Robin's front tyre slipped off the path and he ended up falling straight into the canal. 'I can't swim!' was his cry before he stood up and we all realised that it was only 4 foot deep!

We all burst into laughter as he slowly made his way out of the cold water. 'You need to go back in!' said Dad with a smile. 'Why?' Robin quizzed back. 'You need to get your bike!' Dad responded with tears of laughter. We then continued home, and this story has become something that my brothers and I regularly recall and laugh about. Our cycles continued into my teenage years and never lost their charm.

As a teenager, I had an awakening of sorts when I started to truly realise everything that my parents did for us. Mum would take us to school, clubs, and appointments, feed us and generally keep us clean and safe. Dad would work so hard to provide for his family and together they were the best parents I could have asked for. Conjuring up the memories of those 'good old days' brings a wide smile to my face.

However, those 'good old days' would come to an abrupt end. I remember Wes was behaving quite differently and became more withdrawn and introverted. He started spending most, if not all, of his time in his room and had to take time away from his work. Mum and Dad encouraged him to visit the doctor's and then we had a diagnosis – Schizophrenia.

I'd be lying if I said that at 14 years old, I understood exactly what it was or what it would mean for Wes and our family in general. The truth of the matter is that it quickly changed our family life forever.

His condition seemed to worsen very quickly. He became very paranoid and unpredictable, not uncommon with Schizophrenia. He gave up work and withdrew from friends and colleagues as he tried different medications. This period of finding a medication that helped was unfortunately full of trial and error.

Some meds worked for a little bit, some not at all. Some with very few side effects, some with many. Ultimately, the family began to understand the magnitude of what the diagnosis would mean.

The paranoia has really evolved to become the prominent symptom of his Schizophrenia. Even the littlest things like not trusting food prepared outside of the home or a glass bottle of fizzy drink in case any glass was in the drink to really some more debilitating, full-time worries.

Health was a big one. Every ache and pain would result in high anxiety and a trip to the local A & E department. This very quickly became the new routine within our household and the support he required was overwhelming.

All of a sudden, my Mum and Dad would do absolutely everything for him. Wes wouldn't use cookers as his paranoia played havoc with the idea of forgetting to turn it off and burning the house down so meals weren't something he could help prepare. The kitchen knives needed hidden as he would worry that about hurting himself or others.

He wouldn't do laundry as he was worried about flooding us. It really was endless. Wes was 21 at this point, a young man who should have been out having fun with his friends but that wasn't going to be possible for him.

Those are some difficult cards for him to be dealt. He suffered and continues to suffer a hell of a lot. However, as hard as it was for Wes, it was also hugely impactful on the rest of us. Mum and Dad were so consumed with caring for him that they had very little time for each other.

Their relationship inevitably changed. There was still a lot of love for one another, but Wes was their priority, and his Schizophrenia was all consuming. I started to notice this and began to feel that Mum and Dad were living as a separated couple within the same household because they felt the circumstances dictated it.

Another huge issue encountered by the paranoia was a deep distrust of the organisations and doctors that were supposed to be helping. Wes was terrified that by telling the psychologists and doctors the truth about how his condition was progressing, and how the medication was working, that he would end up being sectioned and placed for a time in a mental health hospital.

Rather than embracing the help on hand, Mum and Dad started to give legitimacy to the paranoias by being complicit in withholding the truth from the healthcare professionals. I was 15 years old at the time and really did feel that mistakes were now being made when it came to his care and prognosis. After all, how can they help if they don't know what the issues are.

Chapter II

Forgotten Sibling

I remember the moment. *The* very moment that I first felt anger and resentment toward my brother and my parents with regard to his illness and how it controlled all of our lives. In the early days of his struggles, Wes was volatile and could be aggressive. He would often argue with my Dad and it could on occasion become physical.

On one occasion, I was in my bedroom when I heard thumping, swearing, and banging from the hallway. It was clear that there was a fight brewing. I left my room in time to see Wes throw a punch at my Dad and, at 15 years old, seeing my 21 year old brother do this to my Dad was unbearable. I leapt in to defend Dad, hoping to protect him. Wes and I scuffled for a bit before Mum and Dad separated us.

We were both upset and told to head into our rooms to cool off. In my mind, Wes had crossed the line and I wasn't going to let him be violent toward anyone in the family. After a minute or so of crying in my room, I hear Mum and Dad in Wesley's room. I open my door to see them hugging and comforting him before I'm abruptly told to get back into my room and close the door.

I was enraged. There he was moments earlier hitting my dad, while shouting some pretty serious threats, and they are in *HIS* room comforting *HIM*?! I was only a child still and couldn't understand why they weren't comforting me, or at least making sure that I'm ok. In this moment, it felt like my well-being wasn't even thought about.

As I matured and grew up some more, I started to feel like an outsider. It felt like Mum, Dad and Wes would think like one person. That the longer they travelled down this road together, the more they started to align their views and perceptions with those of Wes.

I was flabbergasted at this as Wesley's perceptions weren't reality. Not to say that they shouldn't be respected, but they were shaped by paranoia and the decisions made with his care and their attitude to his care were always in direct conflict with my views on the subject.

I remember being told that I 'didn't understand' by my parents and Wes on numerous occasions, reinforcing my feeling of being an outsider to their unit. I strongly objected to them withholding symptoms from the doctors and psychologists because the treatment was based on falsehoods.

I wanted Wes to be as independent as possible, whilst recognising that he would need supported and enabled in order to do so. Part of that support was getting his medication right and that can only be done by having honest conversations with the healthcare professionals.

The idea of Wes having his own home sounds wonderfully empowering on paper. Again, the reality is incredibly different if not well considered. Yet, when the idea was suggested on a whim by Wes, Mum and Dad were totally supportive. No concerns were raised and the idea of Wes living independently just seemed to be taken for granted as a straightforward process.

The house he was offered was 20 minutes away by car (neither he nor Mum or Dad could drive) and he called me one night and asked what my opinion was on his prospective move. It ended up with an argument and I was seen as 'negative'. I gave my honest answer when he asked if I thought it would be a good idea. I responded with several concerns.

How can you prepare meals if you can't and won't cook? How will you do washings if you're worried about flooding? Is moving 20 minutes away from Mum and Dad the best idea? What are your plans for gaining these life skills? My concern was that it was an absolute certainty that Dad would end up living with him, forcing Mum and Dad further apart.

Ultimately, it wasn't going to be anyone's idea of independent living.

Regardless, the move goes ahead, and the result was that Dad would travel over daily at first – with meals. The washing would be taken away when he leaves at night. No preparations were made in terms of enabling him to live independently. No cooker and no washing machine. No support from local mental health team or supported accommodations was sought.

It was doomed in my view. Not because I was simply being negative, or that it couldn't ever be a success, but because I had seen this pattern replicated across every other rash decision made throughout the years. It wasn't sustainable, and Dad would, inevitably, go on to live with Wes permanently.

My voice just wasn't important enough to consider. That's how it felt. I tried to participate in the conversation and offer solutions and ideas for Wes to become more independent, but it always fell on deaf ears. Something as simple as letting him manage his own money and do his own shopping with the benefit of a growing selection of stores offering home delivery, as he wouldn't go out.

As time went by, and I had a family of my own, my Mum and Dad would visit us every Sunday. It was my hope that we could have quality time together. Or to put it bluntly, time with my Mum and Dad where they're in the moment and both physically and mentally present with me in my home and not pre-occupied with Wes.

Alas, this wasn't to be as simple as that. Practically every week, Dad would ask to go home earlier and earlier, prompted by phone calls from Wes. This really upset me because all I ever wanted was time with them. Not a tick the box exercise to say, 'ok that's us seen Stewart this week, now back to Wes'.

I honestly couldn't even take a guess as to how many days that I've lost to crying over the years to the toxicity of the lack of balance found with the different aspects of our family dynamic. To be honest, I consider that my Mum and Dad sacrificed the quality of their relationship with me, and with each other because they were needed 'more' by Wes.

From my perspective, I don't consider that to be true. I needed them. I wanted them too. I wanted to take care of them, and I wanted to see them enjoying life together. I knew it was hard on everyone, but I wanted to find a balance.

I first encountered the idea of 'the forgotten sibling', the feeling that you're being ignored and isolated by your parents because of an illness experienced by a sibling, over a decade ago. I joined mental health forums and did a lot of reading and research, encountering individuals in similar situations. The main themes were the same – resentment and anger.

I was never included in any of the family consultations with Wesley's psychologists or doctors, despite there being opportunities – and there were opportunities. Those opportunities were passed by and missed. If Mum and Dad had co-operated with the psychologists and been open and honest, taken up the offer of family sessions and tried to be proactive with Wesley's care then perhaps I would have felt more included instead of the voiceless individual that I have always felt I was. More importantly, maybe Wes could have found a better way forward, and maybe my parents could have enjoyed time as a couple.

Moreover, this feeling of insignificance transferred to other parts of my life. As my Dad became ill, I started to worry more and more about him as his health deteriorated. Wes being his priority was understandable, as a parent myself I can relate, but as my Dad's son I was increasingly worried that the lack of balance and lack of acknowledgement of how Dad's illness would affect him.

For me, I felt my Dad's physical health should have become our family's primary concern – but the focus never shifted from Wes. His poor mental health was prioritised over Dad's failing physical health.

I don't blame Wes for this. My Mum and Dad would have done the same for me if they had to, because they loved us dearly. Schizophrenia is a horrible illness and I know what it's done to my brother. I would take it away from him in a heartbeat if I could.

The anger and resentment that I've experienced was never blame. It was born from a simple thought – could this circumstance be improved and how? At the end of the day, I was frustrated because it felt like we were just reliving the same day with the same problems, year after year.

Chapter III

Who You Gonna Call?

As shocking as I find it now, I grew up in a home of smokers (Dad, Mum, and both my brothers) where it was the norm to smoke in every room of the house. The thought makes me feel physically sick now, and I could swear I can still smell it! As a child however, being subjected to second-hand smoke wasn't something I considered unusual or wrong. It just was how it was in my home.

I started to become more and more conscious of the smoking in the home as I grew, and by Primary 6 I was fully aware that my friend's homes didn't smell the same as mines and it began to repulse me. I also started to realise that it was seriously unhealthy, and unfair on me to breathe this air every day of my life. By this time, I was also becoming increasingly aware of the damage smoking will do to my parents in particular.

Enter Smoke Busters! An organisation of like-minded school-age children hell-bent on enlightening and encouraging their parents and families to kick their smoking habit! A representative from the organisation visited my primary school class and explained to us the hazards of smoking, the damage it does to your lungs and the other extensive health concerns associated with being a smoker.

The rep explained that the goal of the club was to raise awareness of these risks within our families, more specifically the smokers within our families, with the hope of encouraging them to change their lifestyle for the better. Of course, I was all in on being a member! As the rep and our teacher asked if any pupils were interested in joining, my hand shot straight up!

My welcome pack included Smoke Buster pens, binders, and badges as well as a Smoke Buster diary to record my progress. As a child I thought 'At last, my parents will have to stop smoking now!'. Part of my Smoke Busters commitment was to identify smokers within my family, engage them to explain what smoking does to your lungs, limits your life, and costs you a fortune! I was to check in with my Mum and Dad ask for updates on their smoking and thoughts on giving up.

Dad was surprisingly accommodating. He agreed to cut back, told me how many cigarettes he smoked per day, and we agreed a target for the end of each week, gradually reducing his cigarette intake. I enthusiastically updated my diary and felt very accomplished. I had stopped my Dad from smoking – success!

My Smoke Busters membership card arrived through the post a few weeks later, followed by newsletters and an invite to a membership day trip to a country house and park. The invite was for me, and an individual engaged with my Smoke Busting activities. Of course, I asked my Dad and he duly obliged.

The day was a lot of fun. Smoke Busters put on several informative sessions and provided testimonials from ex-smokers who were now incredibly healthy. There were also several pieces of literature given. Most significantly, free Nicotine patches were provided to adult attendees – including my Dad.

At the end of our trip, I felt really optimistic that I had made a real breakthrough with Dad. I felt somewhat proud of myself too! As we returned home, and over the next few days and weeks, I was feeling more and more confident that Dad was on his way to quit smoking for good.

Dad agreed to try the patches and to continue documenting his progress in our diary. I would speak to him daily about how he was feeling, and we'd use our handouts to anticipate any withdrawal symptoms and ideas on how to navigate through them.

However, I returned from school one day to find my Dad having a cigarette in the kitchen. I was really annoyed, and he chuckled nervously and said it was 'just one' because he'd had a particularly stressful day. Regardless of his reasoning, I was immediately suspicious that this wasn't an isolated incident.

Later that night, I decided to search for his Nicotine patches to make sure he had been using them. I slipped into his room when he was out walking our dog and had a look around. Literally the first drawer I opened and there they were, the Nicotine patches. Unopened. He hadn't even tried. I was so disappointed and hurt.

Unfortunately, it turned out that Dad's smoking would continue for the rest of his life. A life that would be limited in his last few years, a life that would end prematurely. And it was all down to smoking.

Chapter IV

The C-Word

I was 18 or 19 years old when my Dad was diagnosed with Chronic Obstructive Pulmonary Disease (COPD) and Emphysema. Don't know what that is? Me neither! I had honestly never heard of it before. I was at my friend's house, messing about and having a laugh when I received a phone call from Wes.

'Stewart, I think Dad has cancer!' he exclaimed. I panicked. 'What do you mean? What's happened? Why do you think that?' I fired back rapidly. 'He had a Doctor's appointment and he's been told his lungs are diseased!' he continued.

I realised that Wesley's paranoia had jumped to conclusions. A scary conclusion at that. Cancer. I called Dad and asked what the hell was going on. He calmly explained that he had been told by the Doctor that he was suffering from something called COPD and Emphysema.

My reaction? Total and utter relief. It **wasn't** Cancer. So, it **wasn't** as serious as it could have been, right? Nothing to worry about? Well, at the time it really felt like a bullet dodged. A near miss. That this COPD, whatever it is, wasn't nearly as scary as it could have been. After all, my Dad wasn't worried so maybe there's nothing to worry about.

Half an hour or so had passed since I spoke to Dad, and I had calmed down. Phew! Then I started to think about COPD. I hadn't the faintest idea what the hell it stood for, what the symptoms were or prognosis. I was young, ignorant, and naïve but I was about to turn to Dr. Google to enlighten me.

'What is COBD' ENTER. 'Did you mean COPD?' Whoops yes, I think I did! Ok, now I have a description of the illness. COPD is a chronic, irreversible condition affecting the lungs of (mostly) middle-aged smokers. It also included Emphysema, damage to the air sacs held within the lungs.

Breathlessness, difficulty breathing, chesty cough, wheezing. The relief I felt initially was beginning to subside, replaced by concern. Every website I visited was in agreement that the most important thing a COPD sufferer can do is to stop smoking. Immediately.

I knew this wouldn't be an option for Dad. Or rather, it's not something he would be willing to do. *I just knew it*. Further reading led me to understand that it would continue to worsen and could be potentially life-threatening. I started to feel quite panicked again.

Inhalers could be used to help make breathing easier. Indeed, Dad had recently been prescribed an inhaler along with some medication. I was trying to digest everything I was reading, trying to come to a level of understanding and insight into what this illness was and how it could progress. Mostly, I was looking out for ways that I could help.

And then I read the scariest part. The different stages. One stage quickly caught my attention. Stage 4 – End Stage COPD. My heart sank. I realised in that moment that this illness was going to kill him. Maybe not today, or tomorrow. But eventually this would cause his death.

I quickly read the descriptions of the other stages and tried to work out what stage he was likely to be in at that moment;

Stage 1 (Early): Starts off as a nagging cough although some people may not even have symptoms and could even take years to show itself. I felt Dad had moved beyond this stage as he was already on inhalers and had a pronounced cough.

Stage 2 (Moderate): Symptoms are now obvious and serious enough that they start to affect everyday life. Dad was definitely short of breath and wheezed, in line with this stage. I considered that he may well fall within this group at this particular time.

Stage 3 (Severe): Coughing and shortness of breath is much more serious and severe. More tired too. Dad was still working in quite an active role, on his feet all day, so I was confident that it hadn't advanced this far yet.

Stage 4 (End Stage): Most of the time, sufferers reach this stage after enduring COPD for years. Severely life limiting with frequent flare ups which could end up fatal. I found this absolutely terrifying.

I was feeling quite shaken after reading this and decided to head home to speak with Dad. I asked him why he had gone to the doctor, what symptoms he was having, and he said he was feeling breathless, more than usual, and had been given an inhaler to help manage that breathlessness.

I told him I had done a little bit of reading and had read that the best and first thing you should do when you're diagnosed with COPD is to quit smoking. He laughed. LAUGHED! 'It's not as easy as that, son' he said. I couldn't believe it. He had surely been told the same by the GP. Surely, he already knew all of the things I had read earlier?

We bickered back and forth, and I asked him if he would at least try to quit smoking. He told me he would, but I didn't believe him. Fool me once, shame on you. Twice, shame on me as they say. I knew he wouldn't try. Not really. This conversation made me realise just how much I couldn't understand how addiction worked.

It also made me feel hopeless. That despite all of the roads left to travel through the stages of this disease, I already knew the destination. He wasn't going to give up smoking, ever.

Truth be told, I was angry at him. Why couldn't he try? For me? For us? I understand that addiction must be hard, but he'd just received a horrible diagnosis. Wasn't this enough to shake him out of his habit, knowing his life and quality of life would ultimately suffer?

I wanted to tell him what the end stage would look like, that this **will** kill him! But honestly, I was a coward. I was too scared to say it to him. To say it out loud. I wanted to frighten him into taking action, but I was also very conscious that I loved this man so much, and I didn't want to scare him.

Emotionally, I considered that he was dealing with this news in his own way and would gradually realise the gravity of the situation he faced.

Chapter V

Turning Point

In my experience, I think there is such a thing as being too close to someone or something that you lose sight of its gradual deterioration. It seems very strange for me to say now that I really didn't recognise how my Dad's condition worsened over the years. Because it seemed, to me at least, incremental.

Hindsight is a wonderful thing and knowing what I know now and having experienced the things I have, it's a real head scratcher when I truly consider how unprepared I was for his deterioration and death. But I was unprepared. Mentally, as ill as I knew he was, I had absolutely no comprehension of losing a loved one before, that I don't think I could visualise what life would be like if he died.

My grandparents had all passed away when I was very young. I had really no memory of them at all. Dealing with my Dad's mortality was like a glass ceiling for me. I could worry about this or that, imagine this or that scenario but I could never ever have understood just how painful it would be. The reality was beyond the limits of my imagination.

My Dad had worked his whole life and continued to work after his COPD diagnosis. During his workday, he'd be limited to how many cigarettes he could have, and I considered this, obviously, a good thing. I worried that he would need to give up work eventually, as his condition worsened, and would remove the only opportunity for some mild exercise that he would have. That leaving work would make him even more inactive and allow the COPD to progress even faster.

April 2011 was the turning point for Dad's COPD. This was the first occasion that we witnessed just how dangerous his condition was. He had been unwell for a few days with a chest infection and was visibly struggling. Unusually, Dad had taken some sick days from work so I knew it must have been worse.

Gasping for air way more seriously than anything he had experienced before. He insisted he was ok, and his antibiotics prescribed by his GP would fix him up in a day or two. After I finished my own workday, I visited Dad at home. He looked terrible.

Mum was worried and suggested that he needed to get checked over at hospital. Dad was adamant that he didn't want to do that and that the doctors would just send him home as he already had antibiotics. When Mum left the room, Dad said 'Son, I think I need an ambulance, but I don't want to worry your mum'. I called one immediately.

The Paramedics arrived and hooked Dad up to a machine to check his oxygen levels. I don't recall the exact reading, but they did say they were too low, and he would need to go to hospital for some tests. Dad was upset at needing to go but agreed that it was necessary.

He was wheeled out in a wheelchair with an oxygen mask over his nose and mouth. Dad was noticeably trembling at this point and gasping for air, even with the oxygen mask on. Mum accompanied him in the ambulance, and I jumped in the car and followed, calling, and informing my brothers on the way.

When I arrived at hospital, I made my way to A&E and eventually found my way into the triage section. I asked a nurse where he was, and she said he was behind the curtain just next to me. I entered through the curtain and discovered Dad in the hospital bed, with Mum perched tensely in a chair next to him.

He looked frightful. Like nothing I'd ever seen in the flesh. He was already changed into a hospital gown, oxygen mask still on and a drip coming out of his hand. There were a couple of Doctors taking blood and checking readings from various machines. He was clearly struggling to breathe, even with the oxygen mask.

He was also visibly shaking and looked on the verge of passing out. Dad was trying to get the Doctors attention. 'I'm really sorry for all this hassle, I'm sure you all have more important things to do' he said. The Doctor looked at him with a gentle smile and said 'Mr. Patterson, if you had waited another 24 hours, you'd be dead. This is where you need to be'.

I'm not even sure if Mum heard this comment. But I did – and it sickened me to my stomach. Had we just nearly lost him? Was he out of the woods yet? Could this still end badly? God, I had never had such a fright before. I was so worried.

Dad lay helplessly in his bed, and I stood helplessly in the corner, trying to stay out of the way of the Doctors and Nurses. I just remember being so transfixed on Dad's breathing, seeing how much he was struggling. I said a silent prayer in my head, begging for his breathing to settle down.

An hour or so passed very quickly and the activity around Dad began to reduce. It seemed he was stable and breathing a bit better, albeit with the setting on the oxygen tank being quite high. My two brothers arrived soon after and had missed all the more frantic, worrying moments.

We all stayed with Dad, chatting amongst ourselves and with Dad for another short period of time. It was clear to me that he would need admitted to the hospital, at least overnight, and the Doctor returned shortly after to confirm. They suspected that Dad's chest infection had progressed to Pneumonia and that he would need an x-ray and further tests to confirm.

My brothers decided to head home in the meantime, as well as my Mum. I couldn't believe it. Genuinely. Dad was still in triage, still on oxygen, still having tests done...and they were going home? I couldn't even consider going home. I was terrified that he would deteriorate again, especially given what the Doctor had said earlier.

After they had gone, Dad fell asleep. I sat next to him and just watched him breathe, listening to how difficult it sounded for him. I was familiar with his wheezing due to his COPD, but never anything as severe sounding as this. It was noticeably worse, and I wondered if this would be a sign of things to come.

It felt like an absolute age before the Nurse returned to our corner of Triage. Dad awoke as she entered. 'OK William, we're going to move you to your ward now'. A porter then entered and started to prepare his bed, monitors and oxygen tank for transport. Dad was looking way more relaxed by this point. Still breathing more severely than normal but definitely stable sounding. He reached out with a smile and squeezed my hand.

Dad was wheeled along several corridors and at last arrived at the respiratory ward. He was designated to a particular station and introduced to the Nurse on duty. She was lovely. Made it very clear that he was needing to rest and that she would look after him. I finally felt a little more at ease and I started to relax, if only a little! I knew he was going to be ok for now.

It was almost 1am and Dad was exhausted. He told me to go home and get some rest and that he would be OK. I agreed, and I kissed and hugged him so tightly. Then I left, telling him I'd be back to see him in the morning.

I walked out of the ward, down the stairs and out onto the deserted streets. I remember sitting down on the pavement and bursting into tears as soon as the cold air hit my face. A great fear was now living in the forefront of my mind. I was relatively sure he was OK this time, but I also considered if his COPD had progressed to the next stage and how long he might have left.

Chapter VI

Decline

Dad's first hospital stay was a watershed moment for him and his illness. It ushered in a new-found fragility when it came to his health. Although this was his first hospitalisation, it was unfortunately only the first of many.

Over the next (and last) 6 years of his life, Dad would be admitted to hospital at least another half dozen times, ranging in duration from a week to 6 weeks at a time, depending on severity. What could be a flu or a chest infection for him one day could easily be Pneumonia the next.

Each time he'd be in the same ward, respiratory ward 6 of Glasgow Royal Infirmary. We'd get to know the Nurses, Doctors and the regular patients as Dad became more and more of a regular visitor.

Ward 6 is located in the older part of the hospital, next to Glasgow cathedral, and I'm always taken back to those sad days in my mind whenever I pass it. Even when Dad was an inpatient, gasping for breath and barely able to walk the length of himself, he'd still manage to make his way out of the ward and down to the front smoking area. He'd let nothing get in the way of a cigarette!

I'd park the car when I visited, walked down, and would see him standing outside, cigarette in mouth in the freezing Scottish winters. All the while he's only wearing his hospital gown, socks, and slippers.

I shake my head even now just thinking about the desperation and the extent of his smoking addiction. Even though his life was in real jeopardy, thanks to the damage smoking had already done, he'd continue to find opportunities to have another cigarette.

One of the most dreadful aspects of this whole situation was something I learned later. My Grandfather (Dad's Dad) was also a heavy smoker. He too suffered from COPD and actually had a leg amputated due to the damage smoking had done to his body. Not only that, but my Grandfather also died at 66, the same age my Dad would die, with my Dad and Uncle by his side. Dad had witnessed the damage smoking had done first-hand but continued down the very same path. Truly tragic.

There are a couple of hospitalisations that stand out for me. On one occasion, he was admitted to Ward 6 on his birthday. He'd been struggling for a few days and Dad now knew when to seek help. I visited him after being told he'd been admitted. I walked in and I was the only visitor on this particular evening, but he was sound asleep. I couldn't bring myself to wake him.

I sat in a chair next to him and just held his hand. I studied his face and his breathing, and it was the first time I realised and thought to myself that he was this little frail old man. Dad was always strong in my eyes, but I caught this glimpse of reality – he was wasting away and becoming more and more fragile.

On another occasion, after visiting me on Christmas day, he then went to the hospital on his way home. He hadn't really let on that he was feeling more unwell than usual during his visit but ended up being admitted on Christmas night and 3 weeks beyond. Unfortunately, this would be his last Christmas.

There's something profoundly sad at being a hospital patient on your birthday and at Christmas. I often wonder how he must have felt, being lonely at a time when he was so used to having his family around him. Brings a tear to my eye.

As his condition worsened, Dad was referred to a specialist respiratory nursing team. They would visit him regularly at home, checking his oxygen levels, blood pressure and heart rate (amongst other things) regularly. They would also encourage him to keep a diary of his condition.

By the end, Dad was on no less than 18 different doses of medication each day. He had an itinerary pinned to his wall reminding him of times, quantity, and doses. I consider this now to essentially be walking life support.

As Dad struggled to breathe more and more, he became more and more anxious. The anxiety made him struggle more for breath, and the struggle for breath made him more anxious. It was a vicious circle. Part of his extensive medication regime included meds for anxiety as well as steroids and other meds for his COPD. He had also developed a stutter, most likely due to the stress and anxiety.

He had now resorted to using a wheelchair whenever he could. Visiting the supermarkets, where wheelchairs were provided, was an everyday task he could be involved in, albeit with the aid of someone helping to manoeuvre him. A few weeks before he died, we visited a supermarket and Dad was very quiet. Then out of nowhere, he burst into tears.

I told him it was OK; we didn't need to be there, and we could leave if he wanted to, but he assured me he was just anxious. My heart broke seeing him like this. Thinking about it now, I cannot imagine the panic and anxiety he must have felt fighting for every breath. In hindsight, I wondered if he had been told recently by his Doctors that he didn't have very long left to live.

Around the same time, he also told me that he had collapsed and passed out in his kitchen for several hours one morning. I was stunned, terrified. I didn't know what to say to him. My mind was screaming 'Oh my God, *several hours*? This is seriously bad'. But I knew he was anxious so I didn't want to engage in conversations that could potentially have made his breathing worse.

We never, as a family, talked about death. We didn't confront it, and I'm ashamed to say I didn't know how to speak to him about this incident. I was terrified too. I tried my best to make him feel better and assure him that it was going to be OK. Given the circumstances of how Dad died soon after, I look back at this occasion and think we definitely almost lost him earlier than we did. That however he collapsed, the position or whatever he fell into, just allowed him to hang on. Next time, this wouldn't be the case.

In the days leading up to his death, Dad had a mild chest infection. He noted it in his diary as a reminder to tell his respiratory nurses. He had certainly had worse, and I last spoke with him 3 days before he died....to borrow money!

Jeez. Typical. Calling my Dad to help me out, even as an adult. My fridge freezer had stopped working and I called and asked if I could borrow money for a new one, paying him back when I got paid. He of course said yes straight away. I ordered my fridge freezer and that was that.

He called me back a little later and I remember the entire conversation. A very short call but typified how thoughtful he was. 'Was just thinking son, I can give you another £100 to buy some food too, because your food will be wasted now that your freezer isn't working'.

I thanked him and told him I loved him, and he told me he loved me too. This was the last thing we ever said to each other. As far as last conversations go, I'm so very grateful that ours was one of love and gratitude.

PART TWO:
DEATH

Chapter I

10.10am

16th March 2017 – my life changed. Forever.

It started out as just another normal day. Dropped the kids off at school and travelled back to the home office for just after 10 am. To be completely accurate, I even remember the exact time – 10:10am. I was literally just one or two steps into the house, the front door still open, and my phone started to ring.

'Mum' flashed across the screen and suddenly I was gripped by an overwhelming uneasiness - a terrifying feeling, a horrible intuition. I couldn't answer the phone quickly enough. My Mum's almost unrecognisable voice on the line, filled with hurt; 'Stewart….Stewart….your Dad has passed away…'.

Then nothing. A ringing in my ears, a daze. Shock. I don't know how many minutes passed. My front door was still open, and I remember just screaming. An outpouring of pain, anger, and disbelief. Something I struggle to convey even now. I remember fumbling for my phone and calling my wife. I hadn't even thought about what I was going to say. I was sure I was wrong.

Please…not MY Dad, not ME, not US & not NOW. But it was my Dad, and it was now. I don't really recall what I said. She was working in Glasgow city centre and immediately got a taxi home. I sat on the bottom of the stairs waiting for her, falling further and further into confusion and disbelief. I knew it was real, but my mind couldn't digest it.

When I arrived at Dad's house, I knew I had seen him alive for the last time. I walked through the front door to find two police officers standing in the hall. One of them was trying to tell me what was happening, but I wasn't listening. 'Where is he?' I asked. The officers didn't need to say anything, they both just turned and looked into the corner of the hall not visible from the from where I was standing.

I had never ever seen a dead body before. The thought always terrified me, and I had a mental block when it came to viewings at previous funerals I had been to. I looked at my wife…took a deep breath and sprung round the corner.

And there he was. My wonderful Dad, the most beautiful soul. Just lying there…lifeless…beyond help. Lost. My heart broke. I knelt down next to him and enveloped him, kissed his face, and hugged him for as long as I could. I studied his face, his expression, noting his eyes were closed.

I'll never forget it, any of it. He was so cold, so blue and it was apparent that he had been dead for several hours. The paramedics had tried their best to resuscitate him, but it was just too late.

The police officer explained that a doctor was on the way to examine him before they could release his body to the funeral director, as is common practice with a death at home. This was a horrible 3-4 hour period of waiting. We weren't allowed to move him from where he lay until the doctor had been.

What happened next was a little bizarre! Indulge me for a moment. Imagine this, top floor flat with 3 flights of stairs. We're waiting on the private ambulance arriving with the Funeral parlour staff to prepare and transport Dad when the buzzer goes.

The police officer buzzes them in and a minute later, we hear a knock on the door. Open the door and enter two glamourous blonde women in high heels and tight skirts. Dad must have been loving it – I felt like I was in a Carry On movie! Even in the shock of the moment, I thought to myself; 'How in the HELL are these two high heeled women carrying a dead body (safely!) from the top flat?!'.

I mean, have you ever tried to lift a dead body?! It's not easy! At the time, I don't know what I was more shocked at, Dad dying or these two women expecting to carry him down in high heels! But to their credit, they were wonderful. Dad was treated with dignity and respect as they prepared him for the transport.

When it was finally time to take him out to the hearse in the body bag, I was asked if I wanted to help carry him out, along with my Brother. 'Well, I bloody better, just in case you guys drop him' I thought jokingly.

When we placed him in the hearse, one of the undertakers said to me 'You'll be glad you did this for him'. The door was closed but I hugged him one last time before they took him away. I stood and watched as the hearse disappeared from view. Numb. But she was right, I was grateful for the opportunity to carry my Dad. And let me tell you, he was heavy! I still don't know how they did it in heels!

By the time I was home, my head was spinning. I was stunned. But now I had to tell my boys. I knew I was about to break their hearts. It was the most difficult thing I've ever had to do. I was about to devastate them, hurt them. They took it as expected, in shock and pain for the loss of their Granda. My poor boys. One of the first things my oldest son said to me was 'surely, Gran will stop smoking now?'.

By bedtime, I was exhausted. Emotionally drained but couldn't turn my mind off. I was devastated. Slowly downloading little bits of what had happened, contemplating the immediate difficult days ahead and the ordeal myself and my family were about to experience. I don't recall if I slept that night, but it was difficult to sleep in the weeks and months to come.

Chapter II

Lovely Coffins

A new day and for a moment, I forgot my Dad was gone. But only for a moment. Still in a daze, I phoned Mum and told her I'd be there soon, and we'll try and plan what's next. Arriving back at Dad's house with that horrible feeling of the day before was sickening.

After entering I walked up to where he had been laying. I put my hand on the ground and just thought about him. What had happened here, was he in pain? Was it quick, was he terrified? Most of all I was distraught that he had been on his own when he died.

My Dad was such an organised man (a hoarder too!), he had cabinets full of letters and Documents. 8 feet from where he had died lay his life insurance folder. Left so conveniently placed that I felt he just knew he was dying, that the doctor had indeed given him some news recently and he had prepared for the inevitable. He'd noted phone numbers, pay-out amount and details of his final wishes – venues for his funeral.

I called to make an appointment to register his death then followed up by calling his life Insurance, the funeral home and lastly, the daunting task of informing anyone, family, or friend of is passing. Mum and I were in complete silence, working through his documents and personal items. Feeling so intrusive and wrong. It still wasn't real.

Mum then remembered that Dad had a scheduled appointment with his respiratory nurse for the following day. I called to inform her of Dad's death, but she wasn't available. I left a message with one of the other nurses and considered that as another task over with.

The next day, she called me back. I didn't expect her to, and she didn't have to. But it was a lovely call. She offered her condolences and told us how lovely Dad was and that she would miss him. I found it very touching that she made the effort to call me back. I appreciated the humanity and the kind words.

I came across all of his hospital discharge documents and lists of his medications. It was so very difficult to read them. It really drove home just how ill he was and how much he suffered, but also how strong he was.

Prior to our appointment with the registrar, I decided to get a haircut! I badly needed one with the funeral looming. I dropped into my usual place, but I wasn't in the mood to talk and, in keeping with this exhausting week, I looked horrific! I laugh about this now but as I sat down in the barber's chair, he said; 'Jeez, you just off the night shift?' and I laughed gently; 'Uh no mate, my Dad died a couple of days ago'. The poor guy apologised profusely.

Registering his death was another out of body experience. The first time I was ever involved in anything like this, confirming and legitimising that he had in fact died. I remember just sitting there wishing I'd wake up. Wishing he'd come back and help me like he would always do. It was upsetting, I wasn't ready to let him go. I wasn't ready to be without him.

Now we had registered his death, we could proceed with planning his funeral. We went by the funeral home and met with the celebrant and funeral planner. I wanted to protect Mum as much as possible. I didn't want her worrying about planning or payment, but I did want her involved as much as she wanted to be in terms of the input and wishes.

We chose a coffin, informed the planner of the venue we wanted, and she arranged a date and time. Simple and surprisingly straightforward. After, I hated how normal and casual the conversation had been 'Oh yeah that coffin's nice'. Bizarre and detached. They also asked if we'd like to view his body in the coming days, and even more bizarrely, the thought made me so relieved and happy. Literally like a kid before Christmas. I simply could not wait to see his face again.

We chose what clothes we wanted Dad to wear, photographs and poems for the order of service and the music for the ceremony. It was again surreal and completely sad of course. The celebrant visited with us at home and we each told our stories about Dad. Selfishly, I wanted to keep some of them to myself.

I was so eagerly anticipating seeing Dad on the following day at his private viewing. I missed him. This was a strange feeling; how much I was looking forward to it. Unfortunately, it only took a second to realise that it was of no comfort whatsoever for me. I walked into the room on my own and I quickly became the most disappointed I had been in my entire life.

He didn't look like himself, the way his jaw was resting, his face. I obviously knew he'd been in the morgue but the reality of just how cold he was, was frightening and disappointing. His fingernails were so blue. Like a blue I had never seen on a person before. I spent time just looking at him, kissing and hugging him. I'd also written a letter to him. I slipped it into his jacket pocket and put some photos into his clutched hand....and I said Goodbye. I knew this was the last time I'd see his face.

When I think back now, I get really annoyed at myself. This was the last time I'd **ever** see him. The funeral parlour was open for viewing for at least another 3 hours. I could have stayed. Been with him on my own, making the most of the last moments. Instead, I let my dissatisfaction of the viewing take over and wanted away. It didn't comfort me the way I had hoped. Leaving as quickly as I did is perhaps the biggest regret I have.

An exhausting day came to an end and my thoughts quickly turned to his funeral. I was dreading it. I felt compelled to write something personal to read on behalf of the family. I just had to. I informed the celebrant I'd be writing and reading something. I needed to do it for him, I needed to show everyone not only how wonderful he was and how loved he was, but also how grateful we were for having this man to ourselves. Our Dad, my Dad.

Chapter III

Goodbye, Dad

Friday 24th March 2017.

Here it was, Funeral day. Maybe the strangest day of my life – an absolute whirlwind. I got ready at home, feeling silly for ironing my shirt and trying to look my best. Why?! I decided to try and just take it a moment at a time, didn't want to think about the significance of the day. I went by Mum's to meet the rest of the family and we waited on the Funeral cars.

There was a sense of anxiety and dread amongst us all. Then we saw the Hearse pull into the street. My heart sank, we went out and I just touched the window of the hearse, grounding me in the moment and confirming this was real and happening......

We entered the family car and followed the hearse to Lambhill cemetery. Staring at Dad's coffin in front of us the entire time. We pulled into the crematorium and all of a sudden, we see the crowd of family and friends that had gathered. I remember the anxiety and stress hitting me all of a sudden. I began to feel a little panicked and emotional, and I remember losing my composure.

We parked up and exited the car and I looked at all these familiar faces that had gathered to support us and to say goodbye to Dad. It touched my heart – deeply and sincerely. Instinctively, I found myself hugging everyone. I was so grateful for them.

We carried our Dad in and up to the alter and placed him down gently. I hugged and kissed his coffin and whispered, 'I love you, Dad'. We took our place on the pews and the celebrant started the service. My Mum broke down and was sobbing loudly, strangely this gave me some strength. I needed to be as strong as possible for her. I hugged her and whispered to her during the service 'Mum, it's ok. I'm here. Listen to my voice...I'm here'. I remember it all so vividly.

I had practiced my reading several times in an effort to stay strong. Unfortunately, it was all in vain and I broke down in tears – almost instantly. My voice broke and I became inconsolable. I got through my reading and felt the need to hug him again. I turned and hugged his coffin for the last time, again whispering to him 'Oh no Dad, this can't be happening. I'm not ready to lose you'.

I can't recall anything the celebrant said. It was all a blur at this point. I do remember the music playing. My mum had chosen 'Distant Drums' by Jim Reeves, played on their wedding day. My Sister chose 'Daddy, don't you walk so fast' and I had chosen 'Moon River' by Andy Williams. I remember Dad telling me it was his Dad's favourite song, and it was played at his funeral too. My Dad had said he also always loved it.

Then the service was over. My Dad's coffin disappeared behind the curtain, and we'd said our final physical goodbye. The rest of the day was sombre, mingling with family and friends, telling stories, and receiving their warm condolences and support.

The wake was a strange mix of laughter and sadness. It was social and pleasant, catching up with family and friends. I had several pints of beer and other alcohol while reminiscing, but I just couldn't get drunk. It had no effect on me at all. Weird. It was another exhausting, unkind day. I was sure life had changed forever.

'First of all, as a family we'd like to say Thank you to each and every one of you for being here for Dad today and the countless messages of love and support we have received. We really appreciate them.

We have many, many wonderful, happy memories of Dad. Too many to share. Some of the most enduring are from our childhood – fishing & camping trips with Dad and our Uncles and Cousins, and Family cycles to Loch Lomond – plus maybe *some stories that we should never re-tell!! To this day, Loch Lomond holds a special place in our hearts. This is how I will remember him – Active, Healthy & **Happy**.*

However, Dad was a lifelong smoker and unfortunately this led to the development of COPD and lung disease later in life. Gradually, it became more and more debilitating. These past five or six years in particular saw even more physical limitations forced upon him, general ill health, including several hospitalisations and complex regimes of medication.

BUT....even during these horrible times & dark moments, we'd all be worried (!)...but he never ever complained, never moaned & never wanted to 'burden' us with his problems. He was infectious, loving, selfless. He gave himself to his family – he ALWAYS put us first.

And despite the unbearable pain of losing him, I am so relieved that his struggle is over, and he is, at least, at peace.

My last conversation with Dad has obviously taken on a whole new significance given the events of these past few days and I'd like to share those last words with you now;

"Thank you, Dad. I love you. See you later"'

Chapter IV

Grieving

I learned a lot about my own grief and triggers over the first year or so in particular. I started out thinking that I could retain an element of control over my emotions, that everything was a process and my mind tried to take a systematic approach. I tried to anticipate occasions and scenarios that I would find difficult. The obvious ones were his birthday, Christmas, anniversaries. Especially the 'firsts'. Anticipating and trying to prepare myself mentally made sense to me.

However, it was the occasions and situations that I neglected to anticipate that I found most difficult. Don't get me wrong, the first birthday, Christmas and the anniversary of his death were all very emotional. But I *knew* they would be, so I accepted them for what they were – difficult, hard days and inevitably emotional.

In the first year, I actually found my own birthday to be a really difficult day. I missed my Dad being there, even just to call or text me. It surprised me; how upset I was. I would think about how he was there on the day I was born and every birthday since….until now. It hit me hard, even more so because I hadn't anticipated it.

The occasion I found hardest however was Hogmanay (New Year's Eve). I mean, I *really* found it hard. Everything it signified hurt me deeply. A new year, a new start, moving forward and leaving the past behind you. I was devasted that this was a year Dad wouldn't see. A reminder that he had died. Most of all, I felt that time was forcing me to leave him behind.

I was glad to find the strength to muster up some resilience for the obvious occasions and learned some valuable lessons for anticipating future triggers. I was becoming more aware of what triggered my grief and felt a little more confident about my ability to deal with it.

I tried to visualise my ability to cope as being similar to an immune system. I tried to strengthen it with my efforts to anticipate flare-ups and difficult times. For the most part, it worked. I don't mean I didn't have bouts of raw grief or that my grief was in check in any way, more that I was able to take comfort in knowing that I had done all I could to minimise its impact on me by legislating for and accepting that I would be emotional, as it was part of the process.

Of course, no immune system is completely perfect! I put so much energy and thought into anticipating and managing my flare-ups, yet I would discover that it wasn't as comprehensive as I would have liked. The stuff that I couldn't legislate for would hit me harder than ever when they'd occur.

There were two instances that really knocked me off my stride and affected the uneasy balance that I had tried so hard to find and maintain. On the first occasion, maybe 4 or 5 months after Dad had died, I ran into a neighbour; 'How's your Dad, Stewart? I haven't seen him in a while'. I was devastated, having to recount and relive what had happened to a degree.

On the other occasion, I was in a supermarket for a quick shop when I noticed that the security guard was an ex-colleague of my Dad. I said hello to him on my way out and he in-turn asked how my Dad was doing and to say hello for him. This was approximately 18 months after Dad had passed away. I thought I was finished with these conversations; 'Dad actually passed away last year'. I hadn't anticipated this scenario. I felt deflated. Fortunately, the passing of time has at least made those types of encounters less and less likely.

My earlier experience with grief is more difficult to categorise and explain in its own right. It was more visceral, raw, and less likely to be 'controlled' by my 'immune system'. It definitely evolved and continues to evolve. Initially, it was so intertwined with the festering, aged resentments that one of my first conscious reactions to news of my Dad's death was one of anger. Resentment was the 'fuel' to my 'grief fire' so to speak.

Directly after Dad's death, muddled in with being stunned, was finding myself lashing out and striking my door , accompanied with an angry, raw scream. Not the reaction I anticipated. Why was I *so* angry? Why not *just* sad? Indeed, one of my first thoughts was framed with resentment. Dad was caring for Wes right until the end. And I hated it, the inevitability of it all.

Now, just to be clear, I'm not saying this is rational on my part or even fair. I can see now that I was being selfish and unkind. But not by choice - it was how I instinctively felt at the time. The grief had manifested itself in this way very quickly. It gave me, rightly or wrongly, something to focus my raw emotions on in that moment.

Having said that, again with total honesty, I'd have to say that a lot of the resentment I had carried with me and lived with for all of those years left me instantly. Truly. Gone, just like that. It all seemed so irrelevant in the face of the loss of my wonderful Dad. The resentment was replaced by hurt and grief by the end of the day.

The immediate days that followed brought various new experiences and extreme emotions that I could never have fathomed before. I literally lay in bed crying for days, sleeping, eating occasionally then crying again. An emotional storm at which I was totally and utterly helpless to control or influence.

First, there was the shock. I remember looking at photographs, crying my eyes out. My Dad had a cap that he would wear, and I took it home with me the first night. I sat holding it, smelling it, hoping it would give me some comfort. As the nights passed, when I tried to rest, I put it on the floor beside my bed.

Just when I was about to fall asleep, I'd get this sense of disbelief. None of this could be true. As I opened my eyes, the first thing I would see would be that cap. It brought me back to reality, anchoring me back to the real world.

The pain and grief were relentless. I couldn't listen to music without becoming emotional. I wouldn't watch TV in case any respective plots resonated with me. The first time I slept after Dad's death, I awoke sobbing. I couldn't actually see out of my eyes. Never in my life had I experienced this. I couldn't even escape it when I was asleep.

As such, I then developed insomnia. Head full of thoughts and fears. The thought of sleeping and having nightmares kept me awake. Going through Dad's illness in my head over and over. Trying to visualise his last night over and over. It was exhausting, emotional and endless.

As soon as the funeral was over, there was nothing else to focus on. Nothing needing organised, nothing needing attention and focus. It only left the grief and pain – front and centre - and definitely not subtle. It couldn't be avoided, and I really wasn't equipped to deal with it.

The initial focus for my energy was the funeral itself. Or rather the aftermath. How grateful I was for all of the love and support. But then, it pained me how quickly life went on. Not for me at that time, but for everyone else. Of course, people went back to their own lives, but I was left with picking up the pieces of my own. Things had changed forever, and I had to start to digest what had happened.

I had initially taken time away from work, afforded one week full pay on bereavement leave. But wow, what the hell good is one week going to do for anyone? Grateful as I am that I was able to take time, as I know some people won't be as fortunate as I was, it was completely out of question for me to return so quickly. Mentally, I wasn't even nearly ready.

Then I started worrying about what was next. I decided to visit my GP, hoping to receive a sick note for my employer. But I had never had a sick note before?! Do I just explain what's going on and ask outright? Do I go in and try to embellish what's going on? I had no idea of how it worked, and it added even more stress to the situation.

By the time I visited my GP, I hadn't slept in 3 days. I didn't have a regular GP at that time, indeed I wasn't actually a regular visitor to the practice over the years, so I just requested the quickest appointment with whichever GP was available soonest. I received an appointment for the same day.

As I entered the GP's office, he greeted me warmly with a smile and asked; 'What can I do for you?'. Uh, I don't know. Will I tell him my Dad had just died and I felt awful? I hadn't actually thought it through.

I just burst into tears. Not manly tears at that (if there is such a thing!). Squealy, wee mousey tears. I must have looked frightful. I said ; 'My Dad passed away last week, and I haven't slept in days. I'm due back to work on Monday and...', then he cut me off; 'If you're not sleeping, you're not fit for work'. Thank God. I was so relieved that he said that. It made me cry even more.

He asked how my Dad had died, how I had been dealing with it so far and what I did for a living etc. I had a pleasant 2 or 3 minute conversation with him and he handed me the sick note. I was very, very grateful.

Leaving his office, I started to properly look at the note for the first time. The duration marked on it was for one week. 'Damn! That's no good either' I thought to myself. I started trying to visualise what being back at work the following week would look like. Crying at my desk? Making people uncomfortable? Being distracted? I knew this sick note wouldn't be enough either.

I decided to make another appointment on my way out for the end of the week when the sick note was due to expire. This time the first available GP was a different Doctor. I didn't mind either way, I just wanted to get back in and talk to someone.

As I re-entered the practice for my second appointment, I hadn't slept for 5 or 6 days now. Literally not for a second. I must admit I wasn't sure how much humanity a Doctor would or should show, given that they must encounter some pretty horrible situations from day-to-day, but this experience with this particular GP was very pleasant and caring.

She took time to listen to me, I didn't feel rushed, and I genuinely felt that she cared. I told her my sick note was expiring and I wasn't ready to return to work and she said ; 'Yeah, one week isn't enough. Do you want another 2 weeks? Or 4 weeks?'.

Now I could really take my mind off of work. I requested the 4 weeks and thanked her from the bottom of my heart for being so kind and understanding. We then spent another few minutes talking about grief counselling, and she advised that it was best not to engage in counselling for at least 6 months after a death, as you're still in shock.

Most significantly for me, she told me she wanted to see me again in 4 weeks so we could decide if I'm ready to go back to work, leaving the door open for more space and time away should I need it. At last, I could breathe a little deeper knowing I had a buffer from work.

Now I only had to think about how to get some sleep and feel better. Easier said than done! Although I was really tired, I endured another few days of not sleeping well, or sometimes not at all. I reluctantly decided to visit my GP for the 2nd time in a week to ask if there was anything she could prescribe to help me in the short-term.

This was an absolutely huge deal for me. It was totally against my nature to actually ask for medication. I didn't believe in it in all honesty. This felt like a defeat in itself, albeit not the worst I would experience. I really don't like the idea of relying on pills for anything, but I considered it a means to an end.

My GP agreed that maybe I could try something to help my insomnia. She firstly prescribed Propranolol, a beta-blockers (normally prescribed for heart issues but can be used for anxiety). I took them home, felt sorry for myself for the rest of the day for compromising my own view of the use of medication, and started taking them as instructed.

Seriously. 3 days later and not a wink of sleep – again! Why weren't these pills working already? In fact, I felt better (which made me feel worse!!). I'll explain! I felt better because although I still wasn't sleeping, I was no longer tired at least. So, awake but feeling ok.

But that wasn't what I wanted. I wanted and needed to *sleep*. Frustrated, I decided to read the side effects on the leaflet. The first side effect noted under very common symptoms (affecting more than 1 in 10 people)? Insomnia! INSOMNIA!!! Now I had super insomnia!

Here we go, yes you guessed it, back to the GP! This time it was time for what I considered the 'big guns'. Sleeping pills. Surely sleeping pills will help?! Isn't that their purpose after all? I wasn't confident that they'd work and wondered if my grief was just too strong in that moment that I just had to let it run its course. That I'll sleep when I can.

But I decided to try the sleeping pills and hope for the best. Zopiclone was the name of the medication I had been prescribed this time. It was specifically for insomnia and bouts of sleeping difficulties. Surely if anything was going to work it would be these....

I eagerly waited till the evening and optimistically took my pill. Lay down on the bed and closed my eyes. And waited. I felt like I had forgotten how to sleep! Waited some more and then I started to get really agitated. Why wasn't I sleeping yet? Aren't they instant? Won't they work?

I lay there cursing their lack of effectiveness for about half an hour or so, wondering what I was going to do next. It all felt very desperate and then....wait...I fell asleep! SUCCESS! And all the way through the night till morning! Wow, wow, wow! I had never appreciated sleep as much as I did that night and following morning. It actually made me feel really emotional. The tension throughout my body eased slightly but significantly.

Of course, mixed in with all of this insomnia business was the grief itself. I was very upset for hours each day. Crying and having waves of shock hit me. It was really hard. This undoubtedly contributed to my insomnia. I tried to think about each cry as one cry closer to feeling better. I tried to think of each episode of sobbing as a necessary evil to help rid my mind of the pain.

I kept taking the sleeping pills for the next few weeks. As I became more confident with my sleep situation, out of nowhere, I became convinced that Dad had *definitely* been told he had only a few weeks left, based on his emotional displays and the convenient placement of his life insurance. I then had a thought – if he knew he was dying, he could have left us a letter?! Possible. Ok, very unlikely and irrational but I was desperate.

I revisited his house and searched frantically for this evasive letter that must exist! And I mean I REALLY searched. Looked under beds, moved furniture, and even looked under carpets! I know it was extreme and illogical, but it made perfect sense to me at the time.

In hindsight, it was nothing really to do with how likely or unlikely it was. It was all about occupying my mind and giving me something to focus my energy on. It was a distraction. It allowed me to 'remove' myself from the grief for a little while.

Looking back, would I say I wasn't coping well at this point in time? No, I think I'd have to say that I wasn't surprised at how I was feeling and that I was coping well enough. That I expected to be feeling bad. So, in that respect I considered that I was coping as well as anyone could, given what had happened. I wasn't worried about grieving. It's emotional of course but exactly what I imagine every other person in this situation feels.

My Dad's ashes arrived at Mum's about 10 days after his funeral. I hadn't even considered what we would do with them. Truth be told, I thought less than nothing of them at the time. In fact, all they did was upset me further. Arriving at Mum's to receive and acknowledge them seemed like the right thing to do but I found them immediately inadequate for want of a better word.

They were in a carboard box. Nothing special. Just a pile of dust. I felt no attachment to them, and they were of no significance to me – they weren't Dad. Not even a little bit. I kept thinking; 'how can that be all that's left of him?'. The family had a discussion about what we should do with them , and I honestly couldn't have cared less at the time.

Mum however did feel an attachment and we agreed that maybe it was best for her to have them, especially if they brought her some comfort. We had further discussions about possible future resting places for his ashes and Loch Lomond seemed like an obvious choice, given our family history of visiting and holidaying there.

With this decided, we then had the idea of planting a tree for Dad, accompanied by a plaque, at the loch side. This would take several months, and Mum would hang on to the ashes in the meantime. We awaited notification from the relevant councils regarding the planting of the tree and installation of the plaque, poised to scatter Dad's ashes at the tree and in the Loch when the time came.

I remember an unusual thought consuming my mind during this time, and in the months to follow. I started to look at my siblings and think 'You seem to be dealing with this better than me'. Of course, they weren't! They were grieving in their own way, but I couldn't help but feel that I wasn't doing as well as they were.

It caused me distress. There was definitely a loudening of the voice in my head saying 'Right, come on. Stop feeling this way. Man up!'. I wanted to feel better and was jealous of how well they seemed to be doing (on the face of it at least).

It was just one of many irrational thoughts. It put a little bit of pressure on me to 'get over it', an impossibility at the time of course.

I even started to feel angry that my older siblings got to have Dad in their lives for longer. Not angry at them, just angry that I had lost out. How unfair! It didn't mean anything in the grand scale of things. In the end, he was still gone, and it was the same for all of us, but my mind went down lots of different alleyways.

There were friends of mine whom had also lost a parent close to when I lost Dad, and I would actively envy some of them. Maybe because they seemed to be coping better than I was, or because their parent died older than my Dad did, or because they died in hospital with family around them.

What a thing to envy! Crazy. But this was where my thoughts and emotions were living. My mind was trying to make sense of a horrible situation by comparing it to other horrible situations...and becoming jealous!! It was such a strange, unfair, unreasonable way of thinking.

Reflecting on my relationships with friends was another area to focus my wrath and rage at the time. I had tried to imagine what I would have done if I were in their shoes. Would I call them more often? Would I visit them even if they didn't want to? Would I make an effort to dig deeper on how they were doing?

I was so touched by the many acts of kindness, big and small, that I was fortunate enough to receive from the people around me. I was particularly touched by how much casual acquaintances, ex work colleagues and friends that I wasn't maybe a close to at the time would go out of their way to check-in on me. I had no expectation from these people at all but them taking time out of their lives to make sure I knew they were there for me, for a chat or whatever, was incredibly comforting and made a difference.

On the flip side, I felt somewhat abandoned by my closest friends. Some of them didn't make an effort to come to Dad's funeral. Most of them checked in with me on an irregular basis, if at all. In the weeks that followed Dad's death, I was really disappointed in how much support was offered, and the type of support. It all felt distanced and insincere.

Now, I know that may sound ungrateful and an unfair charge to level at someone. And yes, it is! But you have to remember that my mind was turned on 24/7 in this period. Feeling every second of pain and hurt. I do absolutely appreciate the support I was given, but *nothing* was ever going to be enough for me at the time. I was in a personal hell.

As the weeks continued to pass, I considered going back to work. I wondered if 'just getting on with it' might do me good. Maybe focussing on work and giving myself that distraction, something I already knew provided me with a little bit of escapism, might be for the best.

Whilst pondering my options, I experienced a sensation that made my mind up for me. I don't think I had ever, or have ever since, had this happen. My father-in-law had been taking my boys to school in the mornings, partly to give me some time to grieve and partly because I didn't want to drive due to my lack of sleep. I remember waving goodbye to them from my window as they disappeared over the horizon.

Then, I felt a cloud come over me. A big, dark, tangible cloud. I felt so sad and alone. The world looked darker, harsher. I can't explain it, but it was an alien experience to me. I now believe that this was the earliest manifestation of the depression that was brewing away in my mind. . It sent a shiver down my spine, and I decided that being back to work was probably for the best.

Chapter V

Depression

Depression is such a horrible word. To me, it conjures up connotations of hopelessness and sadness. It's misunderstood and scary, and like anything with those characteristics, it can be difficult to confront. Difficult to have a conversation about. And in my case, difficult to accept that you're suffering from it.

We live in a world now where prominent sportsmen and women, actors, and influential people from all walks of life talk openly and candidly about their mental struggles and I'm sure it can help empower sufferers to talk more openly about their own illnesses, feel accepted for who they are and hopefully help themselves and others cope better and/or heal.

There is a stigma within society. I also created my own stigma, in my own head. As I've mentioned, I had no idea of what depression truly meant or how it affected someone prior to my own struggles. The only real experience of mental health issues I had to try and relate to were those of my brother.

With a complete lack of understanding and spade loads of naivety, I kind of bundled a lot of mental illnesses under one definition. Of course, now with my own experiences and an entirely new perspective, I realise that it's like comparing apples with a tin of beans. To put it bluntly, I didn't have a clue.

Thinking back on first moment that depression tapped me on the shoulder, watching the kids leave for school, was definitely the earliest that I recall. It did accelerate my decision to get back to work. I felt that the stability and routine would help me find a way forward. I hoped that it would.

So back to work I went! My manager, whom I'd never met in person as she was based in the United States, scheduled a call with me. I assumed it would be to touch base, offer her condolences and fulfil her duty of care. Well, I couldn't have been more wrong!

The call was actually to inform me of my redundancy. No 'sorry about your Dad', 'How are you doing?'. Nothing. All cold, hard, ruthless business. I just remember thinking that any stability and routine I had, and was hoping to lean on, had just been taken from under me. From losing Dad to losing my job in a matter of a few weeks. The landscape around me was now unrecognisable. I recall thinking that from all of my 31 years of living at that point, my employer literally couldn't actually have hand-picked a worse time to do this to me.

I tried to digest the news over the next few days and started to think that it could be for the best. Maybe a new start in a new place could help me move forward? More immediately, it meant I would need to start looking for a new job. This provided me with another distraction – and I eagerly shifted my focus onto my new task, offering my mind some respite from the grief.

I applied for one job only, and I was fortunate to hear back from them very quickly. I was invited to interview and enthusiastically started to prepare. Then the most peculiar thing happened. The hiring manager came to fetch me from reception, and we walked through the building toward the interview room. She gave me a bit of a tour of the building as we progressed.

It wasn't an overly industrial looking building, but it did have some industrial type features. In particular, it had exposed steel beams. We had reached the doorway for the room I was to be interviewed in and instead of being nervous of the interview, I looked up at the beams and thought to myself ; 'what a great place to hang myself'.

I thought about it so casually. Just popped into my mind, out of nowhere. What the hell! The seriousness and extreme nature of the thought didn't register with me at the time. Possibly because I didn't recognise them as serious or extreme. They felt at home. Normal.

Then, after the interview, I was driving home over a motorway bridge and thought; 'I wonder if I can crash through those barriers and kill myself'. I had never had a thought like this before. Now I'd had two in an hour and a half.

I'd had a missed call from the hiring manager by the time I arrived back home. On returning the call, I was offered the job. I was relieved. I was very glad to have another role so quickly and felt that it could still work out well, that starting somewhere else might give me a platform heal.

Back at reception for my first day in my new role and I again was met by my new manager. As with most first days in a new role, it was a bit of a whirlwind of induction and meeting new people. At the end of the day, I was given a corporate tie. Literally 2 seconds after I was handed it, I looked up at the beam directly above my desk and I dared myself; 'If you're ever in this office alone, hang yourself here, with this tie. It's perfect'.

This was July 2017, 4 months after my Dad had passed away. I was still feeling terrible with grief, so the thoughts I was beginning to have weren't as impactful as I think they would have been previously. They didn't upset or scare me. Looking back, it scares me just how much they didn't scare me then. I just wasn't myself.

I've always been very social. I generally get on with most people and consider myself friendly and warm. Unfortunately, I don't think any of those characteristics were obvious or present during my tenure with this employer. I now consider this period as where my depression started to thrive and come into its own. Previously masked by and confused for 'only' grief, things were about to become really bad for me.

I was a shadow of myself – my mind was drifting away from me. I couldn't bond properly with any of my new colleagues, and I struggled to get to grips with the role as quickly as I would have liked. It felt like I was losing my mind. Parts of my personality had gone AWOL, and I couldn't find enjoyment in anything.

Instead of trying to get to know my new colleagues, I would walk to my car at lunchtime and sleep, setting my alarm for an hour and falling asleep on my back seats. I just couldn't muster up the energy, effort, or motivation to get to know any of them.

This period was by far the most devastating for my mental health. I had no familiar support around me, no existing relationships to lean on when I needed to and no-one knew me well enough to notice my deterioration from an outside perspective either, as they simply had not point of reference to recognise that I wasn't myself.

It felt like I was in 'safe mode'. All of my 'personality islands' had shut down (thanks Pixar's Inside Out for such an excellent way to portray this – I cried!) and my mind was in crisis. I was vacant and only my basic needs were being looked after - my essential systems– eating, drinking, and sleeping.

All I wanted to do was to disappear. I felt compelled, a calling. I kept imagining myself on an uninhabited island, or on a boat in the middle of the ocean. I wanted to be alone, I didn't want to think about anything. It obviously wasn't compatible with being a husband and a father, but my mind craved the isolation. I wanted to run away and hide from my pain

At the same time, my suicidal thoughts became more frequent. When I wasn't sleeping in my car at lunch, I'd be sitting on a bench next to the River Clyde. Thinking about throwing myself in. I'd try to rationalise; 'Why not? I don't want to live if this is what my life is like now'.

I'd sit and read news articles about bodies pulled from the river in years gone by, wondering if those people would do it again if they could. I considered them the lucky ones. The brave ones. The sensible ones. They were out of their misery and wasn't that a good thing?

One of the most compelling rationales I found myself with was; 'If heaven and God are real, why not just kill myself and be with Dad now? After all, when my kids, family die in the future then at least I'll know that we'll all be together. And if there's no heaven, and this is all there is, then what's the point anymore?'

In this period of crisis, I couldn't argue with this 'logic'. It made perfect sense to me. When I'd go home from work, I'd find myself on YouTube; 'How to make a noose' and I'd practice in my shed. Then onto Google; 'How far do you need to drop to break your neck when hanging yourself'.

Then one night I just had enough. I didn't sleep the entire night, and decided I wasn't going to work. I couldn't do it anymore; I couldn't think straight. I'd come to the end of the line.

I felt like I owed it to my manager, and our senior manager, to go in and tell them of my decision to leave the business face-to-face. I decided to get the train, as I hadn't slept, and cried all the way in. All the while trying to hide my face from the other passengers.

Arriving in the office (a couple of hours after I was supposed to start my shift), I asked to see both of them. We sat down and the first thing I did was burst out crying. I told them of the thoughts I was having and how difficult I was finding things. I hadn't confided this to anyone. Their response blew me away.

Not only did they listen, but they truly cared. I know they did – I felt it. Instead of cutting their losses and thinking I was too much hassle to retain, they offered me the opportunity to take some time off. Not just to relax and recharge, but they both suggested that I visit my Doctor to have a frank and honest conversation. I agreed.

Of all of the moments that I've reflected back upon during the course of writing this book, this is the moment that my recovery began. The relief I felt having talked to someone about how I was feeling is indescribable. The concern and care offered, the understanding, and the opportunity for me to obtain a little bit of clarity helped me arrest my deterioration and provided a fresh wind of determination.

PART THREE:
RECOVERY

Chapter I

Medication

Time to fight back! Realising that there's more going on in my head than 'just' grief was an incredibly important moment for my recovery prospects. Until now, I was too busy telling myself that it was 'only' grief. Doing what grief **should** do, making me feel how grief **should** be making me feel. Depression wasn't even on my radar.

But here it was. Front and centre and undeniable. I'm depressed! Clearly. How could I have missed it? Ok, so what's next? Well, I left my employer's office exhausted but with a new purpose and focus. It was time to pick myself up and speak with my Doctor.

Two days later and yes, you guessed it, back at the Doctor's office. By this point, I felt a connection and warmth with the GP I had consulted with on my previous visit, so I requested the appointment be with her. It felt like the sensible decision, and I considered that I was more likely to be honest with her than with the other Doctors.

I was also aware that my treatment would very likely be ongoing, so I was particularly mindful of giving myself the best support and structure to move forward. Having a Doctor that I could trust and be open with was of particular concern for me. It had taken me so long to speak to someone, anyone, about how I was feeling and my choice Doctor to confide in was an important decision. A decision that I definitely got right.

Being back in front of her felt comfortable and somewhat familiar. I tearfully started to tell her of the thoughts I was having and how low I was feeling. She listened carefully and probed me on some of my suicidal thoughts, presumably checking whether or not I was planning to act upon them.

Early on, she said something that made me feel a little better; 'those types of thoughts are common for people who have suffered a bereavement'. I felt reassured that it was OK to have those thoughts. As unusual and as serious as they were, I wasn't losing my mind and I took some comfort in knowing that.

It was an emotional conversation. I tried to remember the pertinent thoughts and feelings, but I ended up just completely unburdening myself, talking for way longer than the allocated appointment time! It's what I needed. Getting it all out in the open. Truth be told, I could have talked all day. I had done a complete reversal – from not speaking to anyone about my thoughts to speaking incessantly.

Again, my Doctor listened intently and interjected when she wished to probe and dig a little deeper. I immediately felt better for speaking to her. Anti-depressants were mentioned, and I was ready and willing to give them a try. I mean, I couldn't feel any worse at this point anyway!

Fluoxetine (commonly known as Prozac) was the anti-depressant of choice. I was to be started off on 20mg (1 pill) per day and increased incrementally if needed, in order to find a dosage that works for me. Fluoxetine could take between 4 and 6 weeks to become effective, which coincided nicely with my time away from work. My hope was that I would begin to feel better by the time I was due back in the office.

My own stigma around taking medication was gone. My opinion and perspective had shifted considerably. An important shift at that . After all, I would do anything to feel better so taking a single pill each day didn't seem like the worst way forward!

Before leaving with my prescription, my Doctor informed me of an interactive online course called 'Beating the Blues'. Supported by the NHS, it was essentially a cognitive behavioural therapy course that would help gauge my mood, anxiety levels, as well as helping to identify opportunities to adjust behaviours with the hope of improving my mood and mental health.

That night, I decided to log in and give it a go. Relatively straightforward to register, I was definitely ready to 'Beat the Blues'!!! There were a series of situational questions, accompanied by some more personal questions about how you were feeling. At the end, you get a rating based on your answers and shown where you rank in terms of depression and anxiety.

As it turned out, I scored really highly on the depression scale (not the kind of test you really want to have a high score though, is it?!) and really low on the anxiety scale. Based on my scores, I was somewhat unusual. Normally, depression and anxiety go hand in hand, but anxiety wasn't an issue for me personally.

Indeed, I was somewhat fearless. Proper fearless. Social anxieties didn't really exist for me at that point in time. I reflected on this and pondered if being through something so painful had given birth to some sort of unexpected positive by-product. I didn't get nervous anymore. What was the point? I hadn't considered that anything positive could ever come from the grieving process, but I must admit, it was a pleasantly unexpected development!

'Beating the blues' also provided additional literature and videos to support the individuals using their course. There were maybe 6 or 7 videos, each about 4 or 5 minutes long, showing different scenarios. For example, the subject of the first video was a high school teacher who struggled to control his classroom and was anxious about attending each day.

Another scenario presented was of an office worker struggling to meet her targets and becoming stressed and anxious. The other videos were similarly themed – all based around stress and anxiety. They were interesting to watch, and I'm sure very relatable for some, but not for me. I wasn't stressed. I wasn't anxious. I was depressed. I was hoping to see a scenario where something happened, a life event for example similar to me losing my Dad, that resonated.

However, It was a gentle first step into discovering cognitive behaviour therapy, and how it could play a part in helping me to manage my emotions a little better. More importantly, it engaged me in the process, albeit not relating to a lot of the content. It was the start of my treatment.

After a couple of weeks of taking Fluoxetine, I started experiencing a horrible sensation. Buzzing in my head and ears, unable to formulate a thought properly or think straight. Even stumbling over words. The best way to describe it is what I imagine being hit on the head with a frying pan would feel like!

I Googled it to see if this was medication related and yes, it definitely was. 'Brain Zaps' or 'Brain Fog' is how they were being described online. Electrical shock sensations in your brain normally associated with anti-depressants. Bingo. I knew what they were and why they were happening at least, but they made me feel absolutely terrible. The good news? They should only last for another week or two until my body and mind became accustomed to the medication.

My return to work was only a week or two away and although I didn't feel much better, the relief in knowing that I had done something about it was priceless. I put less pressure on myself and trusted in the process. I knew the medication would take another couple of weeks to have an impact and I tried to stay relaxed.

The brain zaps continued, accompanied by agitation here and there. I readied myself for work and felt positive about my return. I was warmly welcomed back and given space to ease myself into my routine on the first day. The rest of the week stayed relaxed, and I remained steady and stable emotionally.

As my body started to adjust to the medication, I started to experience other side effects;

- **Some more trouble sleeping**. Taking my pill first thing in the morning gradually helped this improve

- **Vivid dreams.** When I did manage to sleep! VERY vivid at times

- **Nausea**. Not great! But subsided after a couple of weeks

- **Headaches.** Not a great combination when you're also experiencing brain zaps

- **Increased appetite.** Unfortunately! I've put on quite a bit of weight in the past few years!

- **Sweating.** Yes! God, yes!

- **Decreased sex drive**. Damn!

- **Erectile dysfunction.** Damn, damn!!

Obviously, a combination of the depression and my new medication was having some negative impacts on mind and body, but I hoped that the trade-off would be worth it. I'd gladly put up with the side effects for a while in order to feel better.

And then, something happened! Something momentous and wonderful! I remember it vividly. I was walking to the work rest room when I noticed that I was whistling a song to myself. I realised I had been whistling the entire way. I hadn't done anything like this for months. No singing, whistling or anything like that. In that moment, I realised that not only was I feeling better than I had been for a long while, but I was actually feeling **good**.

Wow. I couldn't believe it! My medication had started to work. It felt really emotional and significant. I hoped that it wasn't a false dawn or an isolated moment of feeling good, but I certainly appreciated feeling something other than sad and low.

Whistling. Jeez. I know it may sound trivial, or even silly, but it meant the world to me. It was proof of life, something other than the 'safe mode' I had become accustomed to recently. I must admit, part of me was scared to acknowledge it.

I had a follow-up appointment with my Doctor within the next week or two and looked forward to reporting back with some positive developments. In the meantime, I tried to keep my expectations in check as I didn't want to get carried away, despite new optimism.

For the next few days, I continued to take the medication as instructed. However, as my appointment drew closer, I started to feel a little more unstable again. Ups and downs with my mood, although not extreme, were enough to unsettle me and test my resilience. I began to worry that the moment of feeling good may just be that - a moment. *Only* a moment.

It was at this time when we finally received an update regarding Dad's plaque and tree. It was now planted! From feeling very unsatisfied with the ashes initially, knowing there was now a tree and a plaque dedicated to Dad was a touching moment.

I wasn't ever able to take comfort in any religious beliefs but there was a growing sense of needing to feel connected to Dad. I increasingly yearned for a spiritual connection, but not based in religion. I was over the moon to know that the tree could now be visited.

Mum and I set off to find it, searching a large area. We hadn't been given an exact location (just a sector within Balloch Country Park). We searched and searched for and hour or two and were just on the verge of giving up. I was walking through some longer grass off the main path when I said out loud 'OK Dad, enough. Where are you?'. Just then, I saw the plaque!

I burst into tears as soon as I touched it. I immediately felt a connection to the tree, more specifically, the plaque. Dad's ashes weren't even scattered here yet and I felt a strong connection already. Spiritually, I felt soothed.

As a family, we decided it was time to scatter Dad's ashes. We looked into chartering a boat for the day, taking his ashes out onto the Loch for a more intimate and private goodbye. But first, we decided to scatter some at his tree. This act was poignant and gave me a wave of relief. I now had somewhere physical that I could come to feel close to him, or at least the closest I could get.

The boat trip was sombre but oh my, what a beautiful day we had. We reached a gorgeous cove on the far side of Inchmurrin, where we anchored and set about scattering the remainder of his ashes. No-one really said anything, instead we all more or less reflected inwards. I personally didn't think of anything other than just how right it felt to be doing this, and to be doing it here together.

Watching his ashes diffusing through the dark water was a calming sight. He was now at rest in the Loch, and we could come and visit any time we wanted. As we left, I put my hand in as if to touch him. I still do this whenever I visit, to say hello and goodbye.

At my appointment the week after, I informed my Doctor of generally feeling better for most of the previous few weeks. I was particularly happy to share my experience of my 'whistling moment' and how much optimism I felt in the aftermath. I wasn't as pleased to share my news of my mood fluctuations from the previous weeks.

My Doctor was pleased overall. 'You've had a response to the medication, which is good'. She then suggested that I try an increased dose as it may help stabilise me further. I had certainly experience a reaction to the medication, so I trusted her judgement. I was to remain on Fluoxetine, but with a dosage of 40mg (2 pills).

It was at this point that I realised my ongoing monthly follow-ups with my Doctor were actually helpful in their own right. Not just to discuss treatment, but also on a human level. It was good to speak to someone so openly about my mental health. I would feel re-energised each time I checked in with her, just by the power of speaking to and confiding in her.

I was beginning to find talking therapeutic, and I started to wonder if counselling or therapy could help me build on the progress I had made to this point. More importantly, I wondered if the timing was right.

Chapter II

Psychotherapy

Prior to my own mental health struggles, I couldn't understand the value of therapy in general, let alone comprehend how it could help someone dealing with grief. After all, it's just talking, isn't it? Well, struggling with depression and grief gave me a new lens to see life.

Things I couldn't have understood before (depression, grief, therapy, medication) were of course all new to me. I was learning about myself and how they had affected me from day to day. My horizons had broadened, for better or worse, and I started to contemplate the benefits of certain things that I was completely ignorant of before.

Psychotherapy was an example. I had never even heard of it. Was it the same as a psychologist? Or a psychiatrist? What's the difference? Good question, I'm still not sure! Regardless, speaking with my Doctor had given me a small glimpse of how talking could help and I thought it was worth a try.

There was a lengthy waiting for a mental health referral for a Psychotherapist through the NHS, so I decided to source and pay for it privately in order to expedite the process. After all, the quicker I start my sessions then the quicker I'll feel better, right?

The therapist that I ended up seeing was pleasant enough. She called me in advance of my first session to introduce herself and to find out more about my issues. It was only a short conversation but as with most other initial contacts, like with my Doctor previously, just knowing that I had contacted someone and kicked off the process felt good, healthy, and positive.

Attending my first appointment really did feel like another step in the right direction. It was relaxed and informal, although somewhat clinical like how you would imagine a therapy session. The first session was more or less just getting to know each other (or rather her getting to know me).

I explained what had gone on in the past year, Dad passing away and the subsequent depression. She started out by asking me about my family life, did I have any siblings etc. Before I knew it, I was talking about my early life. Happy times. Sad times. Resentments. Anything that I wanted to talk about. There was no agenda, just wherever the conversation developed naturally, and a little gentle direction from my therapist.

Before I knew it, my time was up. It wasn't awkward and it definitely felt good to talk and unburden some thoughts and feelings. I had mentioned my vivid dreams and she suggested that I start a 'dream diary'. It felt like a good idea, so I bought a diary on the way home.

Reflecting on the session, I began to feel emotional. Talking through Dad's illness and death had stirred up some feelings. I wasn't surprised by this and considered that it was probably how I should be feeling. Indeed, not feeling emotional would have made me wonder how effective the therapy might end up being.

I pulled over to the side of the road and had a good cry, and I felt better. I had come to welcome a cry here and there as it did help to release tension. The session seemed to be successful, and I felt good for having attended. Going forward, my therapist and I had agreed to have a weekly appointment, every Monday.

For the next couple of days, I experienced a bit of a 'therapy hangover'. I felt a little low after continuing to reflect on what we had talked about. Not only that, but I had also started to think about what I might talk about in my future sessions. My mind had jumped and skipped forward to anticipating how the conversations would proceed. I tried to shake this off because I thought the sessions would be more productive if I let the topic of conversation develop naturally, rather than directing it.

As the weeks passed and my sessions continued, I built more of a relationship with my therapist and this in turn allowed me to feel more comfortable with sharing my thoughts. My confidence in being able to share the more emotionally draining feelings allowed me to confront them. It also allowed me to develop and exercise more control over those emotions.

A significant portion of the sessions started to centre around my behaviours, and the concept that your thoughts, feelings and actions can contribute to your mental health and wellbeing. My therapist would put a series of scenario based questions to me and ask me to reflect on my responses for the following session.

I was to be particularly mindful of whether or not the behaviours exhibited in my responses could trigger my grief or depression, and then to consider if different behaviours could have made a positive difference. The obvious example to me was my relationship with alcohol.

I was never a big drinker. Only socially, to have a fun night with friends and at special occasions. After my Dad died, my alcohol consumption and habits stayed the same, so I didn't consider this to be a negative behaviour at first. It was just me being me! However, after a while I realised that alcohol was becoming a huge trigger for my low mood and depression.

Of course, I was aware that alcohol was a depressant. But personally, I had always only associated it with fun and a good time. Now it was a very different story. I reflected on the occasions I had consumed alcohol since my Dad died and realised that although my relationship with and consumption of alcohol hadn't changed as such, my state of mind had. Not to mention that I wasn't even supposed to drink alcohol due to my medication.

On the few occasions that I had consumed alcohol since Dad's passing, I had experienced several low moments. On some occasions I'd just breakdown and become inconsolable, sobbing myself to sleep. On the occasions that the alcohol didn't have this effect on me at the time, I'd experience 'depression hangovers' for days on end after.

I don't mean like your typical sit-down shower, pass me a roll and sausage and a can of Irn-Bru hangover. I mean emotionally. I'd feel very low for days, emotionally volatile, off balance and disconnected. I realised that consuming alcohol was setting me back, and all of the good work and progress I was making was being jeopardised. As the old saying goes, one step forward and two steps back. Cutting back on alcohol or cutting it out entirely was the obvious change in behaviour.

Realising just how impactful behaviours were on my mental health and stability, both positively and negatively, was an important moment. Starting to reflect on other behaviours with this new awareness was the next step. Were there other opportunities to intervene and take back a little more control, even incrementally?

One of the biggest crutches I had created for myself was gambling. Now, I had always enjoyed a flutter on a football accumulator at the weekends, with varying success, but now I was leaning increasingly more heavily on gambling. Trying to find a thrill in the chase. To feel alive. Excitement. Ultimately, Just to escape.

I started to spend a couple of hundred pounds every month, and sometimes more - £400 - £500. I kept this to myself, the scale of the gambling because I knew what people would say. That it was obscene. I was ashamed, but I couldn't stop. I was chasing a high.

Discussing this with my therapist, I recalled the moment I knew I had a problem. Chasing that high, that win was what I *thought* I was looking for. What I *thought* would make me feel good. But that high was never forthcoming.

The biggest win I had was only a short while before I started therapy. I won about £2500 on a football game from a £3 bet! Wowser, not bad, eh?! My reaction? Meh! Neither up nor down. Even a big win didn't give me the high I was chasing, so what was the point? I thought this at the time; 'why aren't I excited?' and I remember phoning my wife to tell her and hear *her* reaction. To try and get some satisfaction from *her* feeling the high at the very least.

It was clear. I had to stop gambling too. It was destructive and I wasn't actually getting what I thought I would get from it anyway. It wasn't sustainable and it wasn't fun anymore. I removed all my bank cards from my online accounts and 'took a break' from the websites that provided that option.

To date, I've managed to control my gambling and limit myself to a small accumulator at the weekends. I've been able to keep this in check for a few years now and have found that my control has improved in line with the improvement in my overall mental health.

This was a valuable exercise in self-awareness and behaviours, facilitated by my therapy. As the weeks continued to pass and the sessions racked up, I began to feel improvements week on week.

After a few months though, I began to feel like I was just 'ticking the box'. Turning up for the sake of it and not really feeling like the sessions were as productive as they once were. I discussed this with my therapist, and she suggested that the sessions may well have served their purpose.

She had patients that would visit her religiously every week for years and some others that would only be with her for a limited time, until they felt a significant improvement in their wellbeing. I did feel a whole lot better than I had in the beginning, had learned some really good coping strategies, and had developed a heightened awareness of my behaviours.

In the end, I did feel that we'd come to the end of the road for the therapy, but with the recognition that the therapy had truly helped me and had indeed served a purpose. We parted amicably and left the door open to re-connect should I ever feel the need to continue.

Chapter III

Stability

A combination of several factors helped usher in a welcomed sense of calm and stability into my life. Medication and therapy, seasoned with a pinch of acceptance, regular check-ins with my doctor and generally the passing of time, provided important supports and perspectives in my struggles.

I was approximately a year and a half into my treatment for depression now, and finally here I was - feeling OK. Not wonderful, but not low. Some ups, some downs. I suppose it just felt like what I considered as 'normal', with normal fluctuations in mood from time to time. Just like everyone else.

By this point, although closely and obviously connected, I could distinguish between my personal struggles with grief, and my struggles with depression. They were two different beasts by this point. In a way, the grief just was what it always 'should' have been.

I always respected it in the sense that I understood why I was grieving, and I understood that it was going to be painful, and all of the other feelings that it would bring. But notably, the sensible part of my mind did think that it would get a little easier as time passed. I came to consider that I always expected to come to terms with the *grief*, but not the *loss*.

Depression though was a very different beast in many ways. Sure, grief and depression both had a lot of the same characteristics and symptoms, but I could now *feel* the difference. And with this realisation, I developed a level of patience and respect for both the depression and grief in their own right.

As grief got a little easier to control and my emotions were more stable, my relationship with depression was where I spent most of my energy and focus. Indeed, after a while, I felt more than OK with regards to how I was dealing with grieving. I could feel myself dealing better with it and it was measurable in a way, and that helped drive me forward.

One impactful re-introduction to my every day thoughts was what I called my 'periphery thoughts'. Thoughts beyond the core 'safe mode'. I spent months and months thinking of nothing. Just feeling and surviving. As time went by though, I started to feel and think of more routine and mundane thoughts and feelings – and it was brilliant!

From 'I wonder if there are any good movies out in the cinema at the moment' or 'that restaurant looks nice, maybe we should go' to thinking of and planning holidays for this summer or the summer after etc. It felt like such a victory and an indication of improvement.

Depression though, was the silent partner. It hid, pulling the strings and growing with my grief. Muddled and jumbled into the same bucket. For me, getting to know depression as an illness and how it affects me, my mood, and thoughts, was a large part of this new sense of stability. My acceptance of depression as an illness, and indeed that I was suffering from this illness, was hugely impactful on my mood.

Whereas before I would literally tell myself to 'get over it, man- up, snap out of it', I now realised and respected the illness, well, as an illness. I use the word 'respect' several times in this chapter because I cannot overstate just how important this was in overcoming my own stigma of mental health.

I always wanted to be in control, and it always hit me hard when my mood, day or week didn't go to plan. I would become angry, hopeless and be really hard on myself. I would often feel like I had gone straight back to the start of the process, and each time that happened, I felt more defeated than the last. Learning to respect the illness was, for me, the biggest lesson I could have learned.

This shift in my awareness and easing of the pressure I put on myself was my platform for feeling better and moving forward. However, the lessons I needed to learn weren't over. There was one big part of the jigsaw that I didn't respect as much. I had lost sight of it due to my focus on managing my depression. That part of the jigsaw was my medication.

As the months passed and I felt better and better, I made an error of judgement. I would spend entire days pre-occupied with how I'm feeling and why. As I improved, I over-simplified the situation. I was less upset as time passed and I thought that this must be down to time passing, incrementally accepting my loss, and even accepting that I was ill.

However, what this made me feel ultimately was that I was indeed in control of the situation regarding my mental health. I thought that by acknowledging the factors at play and the impact they have on me was a way of broadening my understanding not only of the illness, but also an understanding of this new landscape in my head. Pursuing this idea of control was still holding me back.

As my confidence in my stability grew over the weeks and months, and I must say it felt really good at this point, I began to develop some grand plans. Each subsequent visit with my Doctor was more and more pleasant as I revelled in updating her on how well I was doing.

My plan all along was to keep taking medication while it was needed. But I couldn't wait to get to a point where I could come off them for good. It would be the ultimate measure of how well I had done and a symbolic show of how I've overcome and defeated depression.

Best laid plans! Haven't I learned that nothing is ever this simple yet?! In my eagerness to declare myself the winner in the Stewart vs Depression stakes, I led myself down a path of ignorance. Speaking with my Doctor, we had agreed an approach to reduce my medication bit by bit, with the end result seeing me medication free.

I was fully aware of the unpleasant side effects that I could experience but considered it a necessary process and I eagerly started to reduce my dosage in line with the agreed plan. What I was to learn though was that I hadn't given the medication even nearly enough respect for the job it had been doing to help keep me stable.

The first few days were tolerable. I felt dizzy, nauseous and the brain zaps had returned. All in all, I was doing fine. Toward the end of the first week, I started to have regular headaches and trouble sleeping thanks to nightmares. I tried to stay relaxed, telling myself it would pass soon.

Agitation entered the equation heading into my second week. I was really restless for the most part and felt like I wasn't able to relax at all. The agitation also contributed to even less sleep and/or insomnia. I felt horrible but in the bigger picture, I still felt resilient and determined enough to carry on and realise my goal of being medication free.

Unfortunately, Weeks 3 and 4 saw further deterioration. I struggled to stay determined and my resilience was weaning. The differences between weeks 1 and 2 to weeks 3 and 4 were stark. My depression had returned, not that it had ever left. More so that the medication had helped immeasurably. That's how it felt.

All of a sudden, I felt stupid. Like I had made a huge mistake. I should never have come off my medication. I should never have even tried. In that moment, I had come to understand just how effective my medication had been and cursed myself for not appreciating or respecting it sooner.

I arranged for a telephone appointment with my Doctor and agreed that it was best to abandon this attempt and return to the dose that had been so successful in the past. Another valuable lesson in respect had been learned. It was at this point that I decided that I had to let the idea of control go.

I realised that I had spent too much time considering my approach as a controllable process, and that I could in fact direct the variables at play. I immediately came to terms with remaining on my medication for as long as was required. More importantly, I came to terms with perhaps needing them long-term, even for the rest of my life if needs be.

I had lost track of how well I had been doing and how far I'd come but despite feeling foolish for even trying to come off them, I felt I had learned a valuable lesson. I had to give-up on my pursuit of control, or I'd potentially do myself more harm than good in the long-run.

After a few days of being back on my Fluoxetine, I still hadn't seen any improvement. In fact, I was feeling even worse. Even lower. I tried to stay optimistic, hoping that they would start to take effective within the next week to 10 days and crossed my fingers that I would return to the stability I had enjoyed before.

Sadly, it wasn't going to go the way I had hoped. As time passed, it became obvious that the medication had lost its potency on me. By this point I was really devastated. What had I done? Why did I have to insist on coming off my medication? What did I have to gain? I now considered it all risk, and no real reward.

I had rolled the dice on my stability and had lost. My medication had evidently worked so well before, and I didn't even realise it. The defeat felt so deep and damaging – a huge step backwards. It was the worst possible outcome for my experiment, now made even worse by the lack of response to my medication being re-introduced.

Back to the drawing board with my Doctor but with far less determination. I had lost a lot of energy in encountering this failure and the impact on my mental health and mood was staggering, especially when compared to when I had been doing well before.

My Doctor informed me that this can happen with medication, more specifically anti-depressants. Patients may stop responding to the treatment and a new way forward needs to be considered. In my case, I would start my treatment again only with a different medication this time.

I was really low and erratic at this point with emotions all over the place. I was having a tough time. I just couldn't shake this feeling of defeat and stupidity for choosing to withdraw from my treatment. I started to struggle quite badly at work and decided to ask for another 4 weeks off.

My Doctor duly obliged and I tried to prepare myself for what was to come. I knew my medication may or may not be successful and I could, potentially, be about to endure a longer process of a hit and miss approach in order to try and work out which medication and dose works for me.

Sertraline was the anti-depressant of choice, at a dosage of 50mg. This was the highest dose of any of the medications I had been prescribed so far. Importantly, I noticed a shift in how I felt about medication at this point. Previously, I would have found the negative in this. 'Oh, the dose is higher so that must mean that I'm worse than I was'.

But that had completely changed. I now thought 'Oh, I hope the medication works. I don't care about the dosage, just so long as it works for me'. And that was the part that resonated with me – I had overcome my stigma of my illness and the stigma I associated with medication.

The overriding motivation for me was to feel better and I no longer cared if medication was the reason (or a factor). The new-found respect for the success that my medication had brought to me, allowed me to finally accept that I needed it. For now, or forever. It didn't matter. I found myself finally understanding that my journey through this illness cannot be controlled in its entirety, if at all.

It was unreasonable and unhelpful. My expectations were putting pressure on 'being back to normal', and as quickly as possible. The damage done to my mental health simply due to not meeting these expectations was almost as bad as the illness itself sometimes.

My exercise in trying to remove myself from my treatment was actually successful in an unintended way – I had opened my eyes a little wider and found some peace knowing that there was an opportunity to feel better, supported by my medication.

A week or two passed by quickly and the Sertraline started to establish itself. I could feel it working, my mood was changing, and I was beginning to relax more. My troubles and experiences of medication were at least serving me well when it came to recognising progress and measuring the effectiveness of the treatment.

Unsurprisingly, the first couple of weeks were also littered with brain zaps, little bouts of insomnia and vivid dreams, but this no longer caught me off guard. I now expected them, and I tried to prepare myself mentally for the inevitable side effects during this period in particular. I knew they wouldn't last, another example of how the lessons of the past were coming to my aid in the present by helping me manage my own expectations.

The side effects left as quickly as they came, and the anti-depressant choice and dosage seemed to be successful. Assessing how I was feeling after the 5th and 6th weeks was a particularly high point. I had learned along the way that there were many false dawns, so I didn't want to rejoice too early! By week 6 however, I knew that generally anti-depressants were now working as they should.

And by my week 6, I was on top of the world! My brain zaps had subsided, my dreams were still vivid but not as impactful on my sleep, as I was generally more relaxed and less tense. In terms of my mood? I felt really good. I counted my blessings and felt like I had gotten away with the risk I took earlier by withdrawing from my treatment.

I really appreciated how I was feeling, and I had more clarity and understanding of the factors at play. Grief, depression, therapy, medication, motivation, expectation – I had learned a hell of a lot about myself. I no longer harboured ideas of dictating how and when I would withdraw from treatment. I acknowledged the mistakes I may have made but tried to view them constructively. Without the drawbacks, I wouldn't be able to appreciate when things are going well.

Continuing my treatment with my Sertraline, steadily at 50mg, from then, up to and including present day, has been very successful for me. Maybe even more so that my initial stability found on Fluoxetine. All of the hard knocks suffered along the way served a purpose – they allowed me to accept the illness, how the illness affected me and in what ways, and allowed me to learn to embrace my treatment fully with the respect it needed.

Finally, it feels that I'm more up than down. More happy than sad. I was ready to shake off my 'safe mode' for good and approach my life with a different energy, attitude, and vigour. All the more appreciated because of what I have been through.

Chapter IV

Hopes for the Future

There was a time when I didn't think I'd get to this part of my book. Starting to put my words down on paper 4 years ago was cathartic for sure, but also deeply personal. Definitely not to be shared for a variety of reasons. I didn't feel it was in my best interests to share, nor did I feel ready to let people see my vulnerabilities.

The idea of sharing my experience with you terrified me. The stigma in my own head yelled 'No, they will all see you differently from now on – negatively'. I've come a long way since then, coming to terms with the idea of sharing. After a while, it felt like it was the *only* option.

The start of my journey was dark and riddled with thoughts and feelings of misery, pain, hopelessness, and anger. Writing merely served a selfish purpose, the purpose of allowing me to unburden myself. It gave me a platform to channel my hurt.

Sad. Depressed. Shocked. Numb. Suicidal. Overwhelmed. Detached. Broken. You may recall how this book started -

these were the words that I used to try and describe my mental health.

But I wrote that introduction 4 years ago. As my project evolved, not only in size and topic but also impacted by time, my mental health underwent many challenges. It also underwent many changes. My perception, resilience, expectations all adjusted many times, impacted by my trials and tribulations.

As I arrive at my final edit, bringing all of the different chapters together, it has been particularly enlightening to be able to track how far I've come. My instinct was to edit them more comprehensively than I ultimately have. I have resisted the urge to rewrite a lot of the parts I had written long ago for one simple reason – they're a connection to how I was actually feeling and thinking at the time.

And I hope that's where the value is - the insight into that time in my life and the stage of the depression and grief. One of the important purposes that it has served is that I've realised that I would actually write my introduction differently if I were to write it now. Sure, I'm still sad from time to time and I'm still being treated for depression, but they're not debilitating or all-consuming any longer.

With time and experience, I have learned to manage my depression better. And not just with medication, although I appreciate the job it does for my stability more than I ever did before. My behaviours are better and more conscious (thanks in a large part to my therapy).

The biggest difference though? Learning to be kind to myself. To manage the pressure that I put on myself to 'get better', and the unrealistic timescales that I would impose. This of course goes hand-in-hand with managing the stigma of mental illness that I had created for myself.

They say time is a healer and I now believe that to be true, certainly in my case. Dad is still gone, and I still have a good cry here and there but I'm doing well. I'm doing really well, especially when I consider how hard I found it all, and for so long.

When I did make my attempt to rewrite my introduction, none of the words I had used previously came to mind. Instead, I found myself typing their polar opposites; Hope. Happiness. Ambition. Love. Appreciation. Understanding.

What does this mean? Well, it means the world to me. I know I'm ok and I know I'll be ok. I also know that tomorrow might be a hard day, and that I will continue to feel low from time to time. However, I've accepted that, and that acceptance has allowed to me shed a lot of the weight that I felt on my shoulders for so long.

I read a story about depression being like a rock that appears in your living room. You can readjust your furniture and learn to live with it, around it. But some days the rock is bigger. It pushes you into corners, you can't see the TV or see your family or friends. It impacts on you more - It's taken over.

What a wonderful way to describe it. Sometimes it really is OK if all you do today is survive. Tomorrow is another day. Storms come but they're followed by rainbows. That's the way I've managed to adjust my thinking, and it's made an unquantifiable difference for my wellbeing.

My outlook on life has changed considerably. In the depths of my depression, I thought that the best of my life was over and behind me. How can life ever be OK again? I considered this the end of my first, happy life and Dad's death ushered in a second, unhappy life. How can this second life ever be better than my first when he isn't here?

I believed that for a long time. But no longer. Something unexpected happened along the way, my enjoyment and hope returned. I'm very optimistic about this 'second life' and have so much to look forward to. Despite the grief, loss and depression, life does go on. Its never the same but it was never supposed to be, it couldn't be, without Dad.

I've learned many lessons and if I could go back and give myself some advice, I'd say speak to your doctor sooner, speak to your friends or loved ones. You are NOT alone. You'll hang in there at times, but you do come out the other side. You can live with depression and there is life after loss, time will help you find it.

Printed in Great Britain
by Amazon